Dr. Hartnett's book shows that consensus building is both an art and a science. This is a blueprint for creating legitimate democracy.

— Kris Jacobs, Executive Director, JOBS NOW Coalition

Are you frustrated by that common challenge called group decision-making? *Consensus-Oriented Decision-Making* can help! Clearly written and well organized, keep this book by your side and refer to it often. Groups you are part of will function better as a result.

— Peggy Holman, author, *Engaging Emergence: Turning Upheaval into Opportunity* and co-author, *The Change Handbook*

Succinct, thoughtful, and complete. So many groups (including elected officials and government agencies!) get lost in the search for consensus with the best of intentions—this guidebook shows clearly how to get to a decision in the best spirit of democracy.

— Richard Conlin, President, Seattle City Council

In an age often characterized by adversarial partisanship and division, Tim Hartnett's excellent book could not have come at a more crucial time. His immensely practical process of *Consensus-Oriented Decision-Making* provides a framework of participatory communication, mutual respect, and facilitation steps that can strengthen any group of any size. The decisions the process produces will be built on a solid and trusted foundation.

—Dudley Weeks, Ph.D., author of *The Eight Essential Steps to Conflict Resolution*

I thoroughly enjoyed *Consensus-Oriented Decision-Making* in which author Tim Hartnett uses his keen insight and far-reaching experience to present the reader with a truly integrative model of decision making. This book is an excellent introduction to consensus process, a valuable resource book for groups already practicing consensus who want to become more efficient, and a handy reference book for professional facilitators. The content is well-organized and comprehensive and the reader can't help but be inspired by Harnett's passion for his subject.

— Adam Wolpert, Co-Founder Occidental Arts and Ecology Center

Tim Hartnett has done a fabulous job of synthesizing information in a non-dogmatic manner from a variety of fields including facilitation, mediation as well as consensus processes. The CODM methodology is an incredible resource—clearly written, easy to understand and with great examples—for anyone who wants to deepen their knowledge in group dynamics and facilitation. Highly recommended!

— Shakil Choudhury, Senior Partner, Anima Leadership

Tim Hartnett has produced a practical, balanced, and accessible guide to helping groups make decisions in a timely and effective way, using processes designed to maximize participation and ownership. This is a book that all facilitators will find useful, regardless their experience, client profile, or approach to their craft.

— John Butcher, President, Associates in Planning Inc., Ottawa,
and former Canada Regional Representative to the Board of Directors
of the International Association of Facilitators (IAF)

I am so grateful for the timely appearance of this book on our planet. It offers concrete guidance for group wisdom to emerge in decision-making that takes into account all stakeholders. The author presents a wealth of insights and suggestions in such a clear conceptual framework. I feel immediately inspired to re-vision the way I facilitate meetings!

— Lucy Leu, co-author of
NVC Toolkit for Facilitators and
Nonviolent Communication Companion Workbook

As a facilitator of frequent public meetings with City Councils and citizens groups, I value this book both because it puts the entire consensus-based decision-making process in a clear and concise container, and because it includes a host of real-life examples and techniques that can be put to immediate use. Tim Hartnett has created an easy-to-read, step-by-step guide that will be effective for both facilitators and participants in a host of settings.

— David Early, Founding Principal,
Design, Community & Environment,
Berkeley, California

In *Consensus-Oriented Decision-Making*, Tim Hartnett has provided a practical and yet imaginative primer on how to approach group decision making in an inclusive way. Tim emphasizes the importance of both participation and efficiency in decision making, two potentially conflicting goals that are both honored by the CODM approach in a creative and effective way. For anyone organizing, leading, facilitating, or participating in an important group decision making process, this book provides a valuable resource.

— Bernie Mayer, Professor, Werner Institute for Negotiation and Decision Making, Creighton University, author of *Dynamics of Conflict Resolution*, *Beyond Neutrality*, and *Staying With Conflict*

Tim Hartnett's book is a one-stop shop for effective collaboration. It offers a straightforward, skillful seven-step process for facilitating people with diverse views and experience to agreement on outcomes and implementation. This book goes into the top ten facilitation manuals and workbooks in my bookshelf.

— Laurie McCann, University of California Santa Cruz campus ombudsman

Dr. Tim Hartnett's contribution to the world of facilitation and conflict resolution will make a valuable addition to the library of anyone who works with or as part of a group. His *Consensus-Oriented Decision-Making* model covers all aspects of group decision-making and illustrates applied collaboration. The book's theory is grounded in practice, demonstrated by down to earth examples that include group living situations, non-profit boards and work teams. In his presentation of the process and skills, Hartnett includes "shortcuts" to allow any group to adapt the model according to the nature of the group and the particular issue at hand. He also includes communication skills essential for facilitators and helpful for every group member. For "old hands" at facilitation, Hartnett provides a valuable refresher with some new wrinkles. For aspiring facilitators, he offers a definite overview and invaluable guide. And to groups seeking a cooperative approach, he bestows a must-read on applied collaboration.

— Gary Harper, author of *The Joy of Conflict Resolution*

With this comprehensive yet elegantly simple guide to decision-making, Hartnett gets it right. Use this roadmap to turn ideals and ideas into lasting change.

Command and control is an archaic style of leadership in today's business world. Dr. Hartnett`s book is a wonderfully practical guide to understanding how to apply consensus building in both your personal life and the workplace.

Dr. Hartnett's comprehensive but easy-to-understand prose will be as useful in the Congress as it will be in the palaver huts of West Africa. It will become a standard text for multiparty resolution.

Consensus-
Oriented
Decision-
Making

Consensus-Oriented Decision-Making

The CODM Model for Facilitating Groups
to Widespread Agreement

TIM HARTNETT

NEW SOCIETY PUBLISHERS

Cover design: Diane McIntosh.
Cover images: Main image © iStock (Barcin); Background image: © iStock.

Printed in Canada. First printing March 2011.

Paperback ISBN: 978-0-86571-689-6
eISBN: 978-1-55092-481-7

Inquiries regarding requests to reprint all or part of *Consensus-Oriented Decision-Making* should be addressed to New Society Publishers at the address below.

To order directly from the publishers, please call toll-free (North America) 1-800-567-6772, or order online at www.newsociety.com

Any other inquiries can be directed by mail to:

New Society Publishers
P.O. Box 189, Gabriola Island, BC V0R 1X0, Canada
(250) 247-9737

New Society Publishers' mission is to publish books that contribute in fundamental ways to building an ecologically sustainable and just society, and to do so with the least possible impact on the environment, in a manner that models this vision. We are committed to doing this not just through education, but through action. Our printed and bound books are printed on Forest Stewardship Council-certified acid-free paper that is **100% post-consumer recycled** (100% old growth forest-free), processed chlorine free, and printed with vegetable-based, low-VOC inks, with covers produced using FSC-certified stock. New Society also works to reduce its carbon footprint, and purchases carbon offsets based on an annual audit to ensure a carbon neutral footprint. For further information, or to browse our full list of books and purchase securely, visit our website at: www.newsociety.com

Library and Archives Canada Cataloguing in Publication

Hartnett, Tim
Consensus-oriented decision-making : the CODM model for facilitating groups to widespread agreement / Tim Hartnett.

Includes index.
ISBN 978-0-86571-689-6

1. Group decision making. 2. Consensus (Social sciences). 3. Group facilitation. I. Title.

HM746.H37 2011   658.4'036   C2010-906971-4

NEW SOCIETY PUBLISHERS
www.newsociety.com

To my wife,
Amy Cooper,
whose love, humor and wisdom
fills every day of my life with joy.

And to my daughter,
Molly,
whom my love will follow
everywhere she goes.

Contents

Acknowledgments

Since I left home at the age of 17, I have been living, working and participating with a huge assortment of groups. The aliveness and energy of groups has always drawn me. And I have been fascinated to observe how groups work and how they get stuck. Writing this book has been a chance to offer the insights I have gained over the last 30 years. But I cannot claim those insights as my own. I have merely gathered the best ideas I found from the people I had the good fortune to gather with. Everyone I have ever shared discussion with has been a teacher. So I am grateful foremost for all the organizations, friends, community-mates, co-workers, clients and teachers with whom I have shared both hearts and minds in meetings.

I would also like to thank some of the pioneers in the field of professional facilitation. Many of the ideas in this book are compiled from or built upon the work of other authors. Michael Doyle, David Straus, Roger Schwartz, Brian Stanfield, Michael Wilkerson, Dale Hunter, Ingrid Benz, Larry Dressler, and Sandor Schulman have all contributed to a body of literature that now supports excellence in the field. A special acknowledgment should go to Sam Kaner and his colleagues at Community At Work (Lenny Lind, Catherine Toldi, Sarah Fisk and Duane Berger) whose work has substantially advanced our understanding of effective facilitation.

Additionally, several dedicated proponents of consensus decision-making deserve credit for their work over the years, promoting and revising an understanding of consensus process. CT Butler, Amy Rothstein, Tree Bressen, Laird Schwab, Rob Sandelin, Diana Leafe Christian and the contributors to the 1981 book, *Building United Judgment* (B. Auvine, M. Avery, B. Streibel, L. Weiss and E. Nesterick) have all worked to help groups reach for the goal of full consensus.

Thanks also are due to the authors of groundbreaking work in related fields that have been integrated into the CODM approach to facilitation. Roger Fisher and William Ury's contribution to the field of mediation and Marshall Rosenberg's work in nonviolent communication have both made tremendous contributions to our understanding of how to work together toward agreement.

In bringing this book to fruition, I am especially grateful for the generous support of several friends and colleagues whose contributions to the ideas herein were invaluable. Andrew Davis has been a consistent contributor to my understanding of groups for over 20 years. When my thinking gets dull, it is Andrew I go to for clarity. David Early, Tom Sikov, Emily Webb, Skip Spitzer, Betsy Nuse and Mike Weaver also provided me valuable feedback and thought provoking perspectives during the course of writing and editing this book.

This project would not have been possible, however, without the tremendous support of my family. My wife Amy, my daughter Molly, my niece Emily and my ex-partner Sue have all buoyed me with their love and support. When I doubt myself, their confidence carries me. When I need to rant, they listen. And whenever I ask, they offer their wisdom.

Introduction

There is always tremendous potential
for people to work together well.
All we need is a process
that is both participatory and effective.

Making decisions together is a vital part of almost any group. We may come together to form a family, to connect recreationally, to operate a business or nonprofit organization or to collaborate in some form of community project or governance. Whatever the reason for gathering, a group must somehow make decisions. These decisions determine how it will accomplish its goals. So the effectiveness of any group rests upon its ability to make decisions well.

Too often, however, a poor decision-making process spoils a group's effectiveness. Unconscious patterns of exclusion, domination, apathy, manipulation, passive coercion or other problematic behaviors often emerge. The decisions the group makes suffer, as does the group's enjoyment of the process.

Fortunately, the art of guiding groups through decision-making has made great progress over the past several decades. There are now ways to make decisions in groups that are both efficient and enjoyable for all participants. The Consensus-Oriented Decision-Making model (CODM) incorporates these advances into a simple, stepwise model. Work groups, organizations, social groups and even families can employ this model and reap the rewards that effective group cooperation can bring.

CODM combines the two goals of maximum participation and maximum efficiency. Group members can use this process to come up with better solutions than any individual group member could have formulated. And they can do it in a way that respects and includes everyone in the group. Increased collaboration gives participants an increased sense of ownership and a stronger commitment to effective implementation. Group members both feel good that their needs were included in the decision, and they feel a stronger investment in helping ensure the success of the decision. At the same time, however, CODM recognizes that groups need to be able to produce decisions efficiently, so as not to burden the members with long meetings or stagnant progress on popular ideas.

CODM recognizes that groups need to be able to produce decisions efficiently, so as not to burden the members with long meetings or stagnant progress on popular ideas.

CODM was developed through years of personal and professional experience facilitating groups. It is based on the most successful principles and practices from the field of professional group facilitation. In addition, it draws powerful contributions from the fields of mediation and interpersonal communication. Combining the best thinking from these three different fields means CODM can help a group make better decisions in a way that simultaneously helps the group itself grow closer, stronger and more cohesive.

The CODM process can be used to generate widespread agreement in any group. Whether decisions are finalized by unanimous consent, by a vote or by the ruling of a person-in-charge, CODM can assist the process and improve the result. This flexibility makes CODM applicable in both hierarchical and egalitarian organizations. Whenever widespread agreement is the goal, CODM can be used to reach for it.

Using This Book

This book is designed to help you facilitate whatever group you belong to. If you are not a facilitator, this book can help you understand group decision-making, so that you can become a more skillful group member. The CODM process is designed to be accessible to everyone. It offers valuable tools both for professional facilitators and for people who have never facilitated a group before. By carefully describing the steps and the tasks of the facilitator at each stage of the process, this book makes the complicated art of group facilitation easier to understand.

The organization of the book is fairly straightforward. The first two chapters address the basic principles of consensus-oriented decision-making and the role of the facilitator. Chapter 3 covers the importance of clearly choosing a decision rule. The fourth chapter provides an overview of the steps. And the following chapters describe the facilitator's primary tasks during each of the steps. After this, there is a chapter that takes an in-depth look at the dynamics of groups that require unanimous agreement. Finally, the book concludes with some helpful resources for further study.

Throughout the book, the text is augmented with textboxes and sidebars to enrich your learning about group facilitation. There are several different categories of information provided, including:

- **Key Concepts:** Ideas worth highlighting for special attention
- **Communication Skill Builders:** Communication tools valuable to facilitators and/or group members
- **Facilitator Language Guides:** Examples of specific phrasing facilitators can use as a model
- **Facilitator Tasks:** The main tasks for the facilitator in each of the seven steps
- **Options to Consider:** Alternative structures available for use in special circumstances
- **Shortcuts:** Alternatives to speed up the process if there are pressing time constraints
- **Group Dynamics in Action:** Relevant vignettes of group dynamics[1]

In addition to facilitating a decision-making process, group facilitators may be responsible for guiding groups in other kinds of activities. Team-building, information sharing and personal growth are some common examples. This book focuses primarily on leading groups through a decision-making process. The field of group facilitation, however, is broader than this. If you are interested in facilitating groups in other types of activities, some of the material on websites noted in the resource list may be useful.

While the steps in this model offer good guidance, don't let them stop you from being creative. Groups can modify the process, for instance, depending on the amount of time they want to give to a particular decision. CODM's principles can be applied even in the absence of a formal decision-making process. Customize the model as you use it. Apply these principles to make your group's decision-making process both participatory and efficient in whatever way works for your particular group.

The Principles of Consensus-Oriented Decision-Making (CODM)

Consensus-Oriented Decision-Making (CODM) is a powerful group decision-making process. It can be applied to virtually any type of decision in almost any type of group. Whatever the content of the decision a group is addressing, CODM can be used as the process for making that decision. The process is built upon several key principles of effective group decision-making. These principles ensure that a group's decisions are made in a way that is both participatory and efficient.

The acronym CODM is pronounced *co-dem*. While the abbreviation stands for Consensus-Oriented Decision-Making, the pronunciation calls to mind the prefix *co-* as in *cooperative*, and *dem*, the root of the word *democracy*, meaning rule by the people. Appropriately, the CODM process facilitates cooperation toward decision-making that includes everyone.

Consensus and Unanimity

Understanding CODM begins with understanding the term *consensus*. Often people use the terms *unanimity* and *consensus* synonymously. Greater clarity is achieved, however, when the different meanings of these words are parsed. Consensus is defined by *Webster's* dictionary as "agreement of the majority in sentiment or belief" and by the *Oxford* dictionary as "general agreement." For group facilitators, consensus is most useful as a term describing the process of making decisions collaboratively. Thus, a consensus-oriented process is one in which people work together to reach as much agreement as possible. Unanimity (or unanimous consent) is more specific. It refers to the outcome of a vote showing all members are agreed. Consensus is the process. Unanimity is one possible result of a consensus process.

A consensus-oriented process can be used in conjunction with any type of final decision rule.

Once a consensus process has been used to develop a proposal, the group must have a way to finalize a decision. The criterion a group uses for this is called a *decision rule*. Some groups use unanimity as their decision rule. No decision is final unless everyone agrees. Most groups, however, use other decision rule options. They may finalize decisions by voting (majority or supermajority) or by the verdict of a person-in-charge or governing committee.

A consensus-oriented process can be used in conjunction with any type of final decision rule. For instance, a business owner might use the CODM steps to guide her employees in developing a plan for reducing unnecessary paperwork in the office. All the employees may participate and collaboratively form a new plan, knowing that the owner will ultimately decide whether to adopt the plan. Alternatively, a team of softball players might use a consensus process to reach as much agreement as possible on a set of guidelines for adding players to the team. If they do not all agree, however, the team tradition may dictate that a majority vote is enough to make a decision on the most popular proposal they have been discussing.

The confusion of the terms *unanimity* and *consensus* have led many people to some false assumptions. Some have resisted the idea of using a consensus process because they thought it would mean the group could not make a decision without unanimous consent. Others have thought that requiring unanimity is a necessary component of any consensus process. Once the terms are better understood, it becomes more clear that groups can choose to use a consensus process whether or not they use unanimity as a final decision rule. There will be more discussion of decision rules in Chapter 3, and more discussion of the dynamics of requiring unanimity in Chapter 12.

Participatory Decision-Making

CODM encourages maximum participation by all of the group members that will be affected by a decision. This fully participatory process has several aspects, each contributing to the quality of both the decisions made and the experience of the participants.

Inclusion

Including everyone who will be affected by a decision is helpful in multiple ways. First, it ensures that all the impacts of the decision will be well considered. Each point of view on the matter gets a voice in the deliberation. Thus, unforeseen problems are less likely to emerge in the implementation of the decision. This benefit is sorely missing when decisions are made by either a single leader (or subgroup), who may be unaware of some of the potential impacts of the decision.

Second, including the whole group in a decision-making process builds a sense of unity and cohesion in the group. Everyone's input is acknowledged as important, which helps all participants feel valued. Additionally, whole group discussions ensure that all members of the group are in communication with each other. When an organization has separate departments, physically isolated members, factions or emotionally estranged members, a group meeting may be the only direct contact some group members have with one another.

If an organization is large, including all members may not be feasible. In this case, care should be taken to select the people who will be included in decision-making meetings. It is wise to include at least one representative of any significant subset within the organization. If the decision process involves multiple meetings, then there should be a way for the representatives to communicate with members of their subset between meetings.

Additionally, decision groups can include *thought leaders* on specific topics. A thought leader is someone who may not have an official role, but whose expertise on or attention to a particular topic is well known. Including thought leaders helps make sure that all discussion of the topic is brought to the decision-making meetings. This is much preferable to situations where the official discussion of a topic competes with unofficial meetings of people excluded from the official process.

When a group's decisions affect people outside the group, the principle of inclusiveness can also be important. For instance, a group that provides a service to the community might want to include input from the community members being served. Identifying all the stakeholders and determining what degree of inclusiveness to offer them in decision-making are key considerations in many situations.

Open-Mindedness

For a group to work together effectively, the members must value being open-minded. Though we often are very convinced of our own opinions, the successful cooperation of a group is only possible if we are willing to consider each other's ideas as well. When all parties agree to give everyone's ideas a fair hearing and sincere consideration, the potential for conflict and entrenched argument is dramatically reduced.

Open-mindedness can be enhanced by a structure that ensures that each person's ideas will receive attention in fair turn. Taking turns considering one idea at a time creates the safety and focused attention required to discern the merits of any particular idea. This benefit is lost when group discussions devolve into a chaotic and competitive struggle that pits ideas against each other before they are fully articulated or well understood.

When open-mindedness is particularly hard to elicit, some group development training may be helpful. Team-building exercises or more comprehensive relationship improvement retreats can address the background tension that sometimes stifles open-minded discussion. Facilitation of this type of group activity is outside the scope of this book. But it is worth noting

Taking turns considering one idea at a time creates the safety and focused attention required to discern the merits of any particular idea.

that groups willing to devote time and resources to team-building are likely to experience greater openness in decision-making.

Empathy

Empathy is a vital part of any functional group process. For people to work well together, they must be able to understand each other. And if they can understand not only the words and ideas expressed, but also the underlying feelings and needs, then a real sense of connection can develop. While connection may not be an overt goal of a particular group, the fact remains that people cooperate better and feel more motivated to contribute when they feel more connected to the group. An empathetic process is one where group members take time to clearly express their understanding of each other. It not only helps avoid the miscommunication of ideas; it strengthens the relationships between group members.

Collaboration

Collaborative group discussions are often the best way to devise solutions to complex problems. Each person has both a unique perspective and a unique genius to bring to problem solving. When they work together poorly, too many cooks can spoil the broth. But when members successfully collaborate, the group can come up with creative solutions that no single person was capable of concocting.

The process of collaboration requires that participants release any entrenched positions they may have held prior to the meeting. They are directed by the facilitator to identify all the underlying needs and concerns of each party affected by the decision. The resulting solution is therefore the group's best attempt to meet as many needs as possible. This is in contrast to non-collaborative decision-making, where one solution that meets certain needs is pitted against another solution that meets competing needs.

Shared Ownership

Participatory decision-making fosters a sense of shared ownership of the resulting decisions. When group members are included; when they are heard with an open mind; when both their thoughts and their feelings are clearly understood and when their ideas are woven into a collaborative solution they are likely to feel a shared responsibility for the decisions reached. This shared ownership of the decision often results in a heightened commitment by all group members to ensure successful implementation of the decision. Apathy, passive-aggressive behavior and other forms of undermining become far less likely. Instead, a shared internal motivation to succeed becomes the dominant dynamic.

Marcel lived in a large household of grad students near the University of California in Santa Cruz. The group of renters shared a large yard that, according to the lease, was the responsibility of the tenants to maintain. Marcel considered this duty to be sadly neglected, and he decided to take some leadership to solve the problem. He crafted a list of landscaping tasks and constructed a chore wheel to distribute responsibility for these tasks equally to all household members. He posted the chore wheel where everyone could see it, along with a note on the wall asking for everyone's cooperation.

Unfortunately, after several weeks it became apparent that few people were actually doing any yard work. Marcel could not understand why. His system was intended to be fair and reasonable. When he pressed people to do their share, some housemates actually got angry with him. "You're not the landlord," Juno said.

Marcel was angry too. He considered moving out of the household. But a friend convinced him to call for a house meeting and try to use a participatory decision-making process. In the meeting, Marcel apologized for trying to solve the problem himself and asked the group to come up with a solution. The resulting inclusive discussion identified that some household members felt their extra contributions in the kitchen should offset their yard work responsibilities. Others were willing to mow the lawn, but had no idea how to prune trees or differentiate weeds from perennial herbs. They listened to each other and began to generate a way to adapt the concept of a chore wheel until everyone felt a genuine willingness to make help make the system work.

FIGURE 1.1. Summary of Participatory Decision-Making Principles[1]

Principle	Participatory Decision-Making	Non-Participatory Decision-Making
Inclusion	All group members and as many stakeholders as possible are present. Each person has a chance to speak and be heard. The needs of stakeholders not present are considered.	Key people affected by a decision are not present for the discussion. Some voices dominate, while others are silent. Those not attending are not represented.
Open-Mindedness	Participants are encouraged to be open-minded. Everyone is asked to consider all perspectives. Unique points of view are valued.	Participants represent fixed positions and argue the merits of their own point of view. Only popular ideas are worth discussing.
Empathy	Effort is made to provide participants the experience of being understood. This applies both to their ideas and feelings.	The discussion focuses on the ideas being debated, without concern for offering empathy to the participants.
Collaboration	Proposals are built with everyone contributing, and designed to meet as many stakeholder needs as possible. All concerns are considered important.	Proposals generated by individuals or sub-groups compete to win sufficient approval to become adopted by the group. Each proposal mainly addresses the concerns of its advocates.
Shared Ownership	All participants, having jointly developed a proposal, share a common motivation to make implementation of the resulting decision succeed. The group leadership participates in the discussion.	The group leadership makes decisions without participating in the discussion. Advocates of a proposal are motivated during implementation. But others may be apathetic or possibly undermine successful implementation.

Efficient Decision-Making

Another fundamental value of the CODM process is that group decision-making must be efficient as well as participatory. Without an effective process, a group trying for greater participation is likely to suffer a serious loss of efficiency. Eventually, groups that cannot make decisions effectively are likely to frustrate members so much that participation declines or the group fails at its mission. Members begin to dread or avoid meetings or show up in body only. Groups cannot maintain high levels of participation without operating efficiently.

Greater participation does take time. If all participants have a voice, each voice deserves to be heard and understood. The time invested in respectful listening, however, does not indicate a loss of efficiency. It can improve collaboration and strengthen group cohesion in valuable ways. Time spent improving the group atmosphere is not wasted. In fact, this time may be "harvested on the back end." Finalizing and implementing decisions may go much more smoothly when a little time is invested in high-participation group discussions.

The final key to efficient decision-making is clarity about how a decision becomes finalized.

Efficiency is lost only when group participation is poorly managed. Bickering, polarizing, grandstanding, withholding and various other non-collaborative interactions are the real time wasters. Groups must be structured and facilitated well enough to avoid frustrating the members to the point where they no longer want to participate.

Fortunately, with effective structure, skillful facilitation and a clear decision rule, more participation does not have to mean less efficiency. Even very large meetings can reap the benefits of a participatory process while remaining efficient. The keys to an efficient process lie in the following principles.

Effective Meeting Structure

An effective meeting structure guides a group through decision-making with clear milestones and transition points. It coordinates the group members to focus together on each important stage of decision-making. It also prevents the chaos and dysfunctional dynamics that can wreak havoc when there is no structure to a discussion. Even naturally skilled facilitators can easily get overwhelmed trying to guide a group without a clearly structured process.

CODM is a stepwise structure for guiding a group through a decision-making discussion. It can help a group navigate through even the most challenging decisions. It is not, however, an overall structure for leading groups. Groups do many things other than make decisions. Those other functions may be well served by other structures, or perhaps by unstructured interactions. The CODM process is not intended to cover all aspects of group facilitation. Its use is specific to the task of facilitating group decision-making.

Skillful Facilitation

A skillful facilitator can successfully use an effective meeting structure to guide the group to a satisfying result. Without competent facilitation, a group may not be able to follow a structure, no matter how well that structure is designed. It is the combination of good structure and skillful facilitation that is essential. As we will see, skillful facilitation also includes preparing well for group discussions. The next chapter discusses the general qualities and responsibilities of a group facilitator.

Clear Decision Rule

The final key to efficient decision-making is clarity about how a decision becomes finalized. Different groups have different final decision rules. Sometimes the determining criterion is clear; sometimes it is murky. The options fall along a well-known spectrum. In hierarchically structured organizations, final decision-making authority rests with a particular person-in-charge. Sometimes the person is actually a small group or executive committee. In democratic organizations the authority is held by the group and exercised through either majority rule, supermajority or in some cases unanimity.

FIGURE 1.2. Summary of Efficient Decision-Making Principles

Principle	Efficient Decision-Making	Non-Efficient Decision-Making
Effective Meeting Structure	Group uses a stepwise model that keeps the discussion progressively on track toward a decision. Each popular alternative is given a turn for focused consideration.	Group has extended periods of confusion about the topic. Multiple issues compete for attention. Convergence of ideas is left up to chance.
Skillful Facilitation	The facilitator is prepared, skilled and empowered to shepherd the process, keeping the group inspired and on track toward a decision in a safe, supportive atmosphere.	The facilitator allows non-productive or non-collaborative behavior to predominate.
Clear Decision Rule	Group has an established default decision rule.	Group's decision rule is vague or the group must establish a new decision criterion for each decision.

The CODM process can be used with any of these final decision-making authority criteria. The benefits of efficiency and participation are useful in any case. The different options each carry their own pros and cons. These are outlined in Chapter 4. No decision-making process (including CODM) will be effective, however, when the group's final decision rule is not clearly understood by the participants.

Summary

Consensus-Oriented Decision-Making is a process any group can use to produce decisions made both efficiently and with a high degree of participation. This combination enables groups to reap the many benefits of working together, while ensuring that such collaboration is enjoyable rather than frustrating.

The CODM
Facilitator Role

The great leaders are like the best conductors—they reach
beyond the notes to reach the magic in the players.

Blaine Lee

If you are reading this book, it is probably because you want the groups you
know to function better. Group facilitation may be your profession, a part
of your job or a volunteer interest. If you are not a facilitator, you may just
want to understand more about how groups work. Whatever the context,
learning to facilitate empowers you to offer a valuable skill. By providing
this skill in the service of a group, you can be a vital catalyst. You can use
your role to create a chance for everyone in the group to contribute their
talents as well. And as you help your group collaborate in decision-making,
you are likely to be helping your fellow group members grow more connected and helping your group become more cohesive.

As you provide this valuable service, you may find that you may grow
as well. The role of facilitator can be very challenging. It demands that you
deal effectively with your own emotions so that you can stay available to the
group. It demands that you treat everyone with respect and compassion.
But it also demands that you deal effectively with people when their behavior is not helpful to the group. Facilitators must sometimes be inspirational,

and sometimes very practical. You must be able to model all the qualities you want to foster in the groups you lead. The challenge can beckon you to keep growing as a person, so that you can function with ever increasing grace.

Developing facilitation skills takes time and experience. Inevitably, there will be times when you will flounder. You may feel lost, overwhelmed or frustrated. If your heart is in it, however, most groups will help you succeed. After all, your success as a facilitator will ultimately help the group. Mistakes are okay, as long as you keep paying attention and are willing to make adjustments. There will always be some trial and error in the learning process. With the following principles in mind, however, even a novice facilitator can get started in the right direction.

Group Leadership

Understanding the role of a group facilitator requires some discussion of group leadership in general. The facilitator has the official role of guiding a group through a meeting or decision-making process. The group, however, may have other official leadership positions as well. Depending on how it is organized, a group may have a president, chairperson, director(s), business owner, manager or other type of designated leader or leaders. Alternatively, some groups have no official leadership roles. Regardless of who occupies specific roles, however, group leadership is a vital function.

Egalitarian Leadership

Good leadership involves "thinking about the whole group." This function is not limited, however, to people holding an official leadership position. In fact, anyone in the group who is thinking about the whole group could be considered an unofficial leader. When a group member asks herself, "What is the group needing now?" she is practicing leadership. A designated facilitator may be expected to function this way. But groups work best when all the members realize they have the power to take this perspective as well.

Group cooperation can increase when participants are encouraged to adopt this more egalitarian definition of leadership. No one need feel excluded from the opportunity to assist the group. Just because a member does not have an official role does not mean they do not have good ideas that could help the group. Openly encouraging participants to think about the whole group benefits a facilitator in several ways:

- There is less resistance to the perceived power a facilitator may have.
- Group members are less passive.
- More intelligences are available whenever the group gets stuck.
- Participants demonstrate more concern for one another.

An important consideration in egalitarian leadership is how participants can work *with* rather than *against* the facilitator. If a participant engages in a power struggle to assert his ideas in competition with the facilitator, he is probably not thinking clearly about the needs of the whole group. It is more useful to offer ideas in ways that help the facilitator make good choices. Then the group does not get distracted from their work by the dynamics of a leadership challenge.

I was facilitating a meeting to address sexism on a college campus when I misheard a comment about date rape made by a female student. When I tried to reflect back her point of view, the group thought I was expressing my personal opinion. Several audience members registered distinct disagreement with that opinion. I did not understand, however, why they seemed to be challenging me personally. I could feel the tension in the room mount. Some were very uncomfortable with their facilitator being confronted. Others shared the demand for an explanation. I fumbled to defend myself, without realizing how I had been misunderstood. I got more and more inarticulate as it appeared that I was only putting my foot deeper into my mouth.

Fortunately, I caught the eye of a student near me. She flashed me her notebook page on which she had written in large letters "LET'S BREAK." I took her advice and called for a brief intermission. During the break I was able to identify the mistake and figure out how to proceed. The break was just what both the group and I needed. Though the student had no official role, she was a leader of the group at a moment when I was lost and confused. She was the one who figured out what we all needed.

A designated facilitator can provide clarity in directing the process of the group more effectively than a chorus of unofficial group members. Knowing this, however, group members without an official role can still exercise leadership. They can think about how the facilitator can be supported to serve the group well. They can call attention to the needs of the group without blaming or criticizing either the facilitator or other members of the group. When facilitators can cultivate this type of leadership within the group, meetings can be very enjoyable.

Facilitative Leadership

Facilitative leadership is an emerging paradigm in organizational management.[1] A facilitative leader is someone who leads by fostering collaboration. This is in contrast to traditional hierarchical management paradigms and more directive styles. The CODM process is a valuable tool for facilitative leaders. It offers a way to help groups reach collaborative decisions with maximum participation, efficiency and shared ownership. A facilitative leader, however, extends the principles behind CODM to a broader range of

FIGURE 2.1. Comparing Leadership Styles

Situation	Facilitative Leadership Style	Directive Leadership Style
Complaints about stressful working conditions	Facilitate group discussion of the source of stress and possible solutions.	Shift individual responsibilities to reduce the stress on the people complaining. Or give pep talk on how to deal better with stress.
People not complying with existing policies	Facilitate group discussion on the root causes of non-compliance. Consider systemic changes.	Institute better oversight and enforce compliance.
Conflict between co-workers	Facilitate discussion of possible underlying dynamics and unmet needs within the organization.	Adjudicate and request that each party try better to cooperate with each other.

management duties. Rather than asking, "How do I set goals, delegate tasks and hold people accountable?" the facilitative leader asks, "How do I foster the group's ability to envision, collaborate and implement projects they can own themselves?"

Group Leaders and Group Facilitators

If a group has a designated leader, that person may be the one who facilitates meetings and group decision-making. Usually it is preferable, however, for someone else to act as facilitator. Separating these roles can be helpful for several reasons:

- The leader may not have strong facilitation skills.
- The leader may have difficulty staying neutral.
- The leader may have a more formal, less empathetic relationship to the others.
- The leader may be able to listen more carefully when she is not simultaneously facilitating.
- The issue may be so controversial that an outside facilitator is needed.
- The leader may be better able to provide important information to the group when she is not simultaneously facilitating.

Some leaders may be hesitant to yield the role of facilitator to someone else. If they can learn to trust a facilitator, however, they often enjoy being able to participate in discussions as a group member. The group may also enjoy the decreased power differential between the participants and the leader when they all have equal footing in a discussion. A more collegial feeling can develop during a meeting even if the final decision power still rests with the leader.

Facilitators from outside of the group can also be useful. Sometimes there is no group member that can be neutral enough on the content of an issue to serve well as a facilitator. Alternatively, available group members may not have sufficient skill to take on the role. An outside facilitator can provide valuable facilitation expertise and a clearly neutral approach. When successful, outside facilitators can help groups greatly increase their efficiency in decision-making, saving valuable group time and organizational resources.

Dual Roles

When an outside facilitator is not used, the role is occupied by either a group leader or another group member. This means that the facilitator may sometimes have to step out of one role in order to speak to the group in the other role. In other words, the facilitator may choose to take off his facilitator hat and put on his group member hat in order to speak from an individual perspective. The group benefits when this role change is clearly articulated. And it is less confusing when hats are not changed too often. For this reason, the strength of each person's opinions about an issue should be a factor in the choice of who facilitates a decision. A person who feels less need to express personal opinions may be more effective as a facilitator.

General Qualities of Effective Facilitators

There are some general qualities that skillful facilitators must learn to embody. Rather than specific tasks, these qualities constitute an effective style of operating as a facilitator. The individual personalities of different facilitators may vary widely. But the qualities described here are essential to function well in the role.

Process Focused/Content Neutral

A group facilitator guides the decision-making process. It is important, however, for the facilitator to stay neutral on the content of a group's decisions. No one wants a facilitator who is biased toward a particular proposal. Any perceived bias may diminish participants' trust that the process being used is fair. Some group members may accommodate to the facilitator's perspective, and others may resist. A facilitator who stays neutral on the content of the discussion ensures that the group decision is truly representative of the group and not a result of biased leadership.

While facilitators are neutral on content, however, they can be very assertive about process. Their job is to continually shepherd the group through the steps necessary to make a decision. The attention they place on the process helps ensure that these steps are traversed in a way that maintains a positive group experience.

It is vital to understand the difference between process and content. Figure 2.2 below can help make the distinction clear. The facilitator focuses on the group's process while the group focuses on the content of the discussion. The facilitator actively guides, suggests and asserts the direction of the decision-making process. If this guidance is resisted, the facilitator must listen and respond to feedback. Then, she can use the feedback to reestablish an acceptable process, one that allows the group to refocus on the content of the discussion.

FIGURE 2.2. Content vs. Process

Content	Process
What we are talking about	The way we talk about it
The problem we are trying to solve	The steps we take to find a solution
The proposal we develop	The way we develop the proposal
The final decision	The means of finalizing the decision

Staying focused on the group process is sometimes challenging. You may be so tempted to help your group achieve its goal that you forget that the journey is as important as the destination. The facilitator's job is to make sure the road to a decision does not damage the group. Even if the group does not reach its goals, the facilitator is successful whenever she has helped the process to remain respectful and collaborative.

Empowered

Facilitators hold a pivotal role in a group. They must use the authority of this role to ensure a successful group process. To be effective, they must make clear suggestions about how to proceed. A good facilitator allows the group to stay focused on deciding the issue at hand (content of the decision). Meanwhile, the facilitator confidently guides the group on how the process will unfold.

Asserting yourself in a group can be scary. It is impossible to please everyone at all times. Sometimes you must take action, on behalf of the group, despite opposition from one or more participants. Group members who disagree may criticize you. With enough grace, non-defensiveness and communication skill, you can usually regain the cooperation of resistant participants. But there will be times when you must rely primarily on your own confidence to carry you, until you reestablish the whole group's cooperation.

A facilitator who is hesitant to act may leave the group wallowing, without clear direction. The vacuum of leadership may attract attempts for dominance of the group from members who may have assertive personalities or who hold leadership positions, but are not skilled in facilitation. If a participant appears to have taken control of the process from the facilitator, other participants may try to compete for control as well. The group's atmosphere and progress toward a decision will then be hampered by the ensuing power struggle.

Thus, it is important to act when the group needs facilitation. The dilemma is that sometimes the group will need facilitation, but you will not know what to do! There are always two options available. One, you can make a choice, knowing that if it does not work well, you can always change course. Or two, you can pose a question to the group. Both require that you be responsive to group input, either before or immediately after you make a process decision.

Responsive

Skillful facilitators use their authority to direct the process with close attention to how the group is responding to each direction they offer. Responsiveness to the group is vital. It helps a facilitator maintain the authority to lead. Groups will either rebel or fall passive when a facilitator's choices are out of sync with the group. No facilitator can be expected to guess correctly about what needs to happen at each stage of a group process. Fortunately, group members are likely to forgive any mistaken initiatives if the facilitator is observant enough to recognize that a misstep was made.

Facilitators can ensure greater responsiveness by periodically soliciting feedback from the group. When a facilitator is unsure about how to proceed, he can pose a question to the group for either comments or a vote. For instance, a facilitator may ask the group members if they are ready to close discussion of one topic and move to the next. The question can be framed as an either/or choice. Or it can be more open, such as "What do people think needs to happen next?" Since not all group members may agree, they depend on the facilitator to assess the feedback and then choose what step would be in the best interest of the whole group.

Inspirational

A skillful facilitator must inspire the group. Sometimes, difficult group dynamics have drained group members of confidence that they can successfully work together. Past failures to cooperate may leave feelings of distrust or even contempt between participants. When people are convinced that their efforts are hopeless, they may not evidence the motivation it takes to succeed. Thus, the facilitator who can inspire a group with confidence about the potential to successfully work together will get the best results.

The good news is that there is always tremendous potential for people to work together well. Regardless of past difficulties, the advantages inherent in coordinating our efforts can vastly exceed the alternative (pursuing independent and potentially competing efforts). All we need is a process that is participatory and effective. The more experience the facilitator has in using an effective process, the more confidence she can express to the group that success is possible.

The Facilitator's Primary Responsibilities

In addition to the general qualities listed above, the facilitator has multiple ongoing responsibilities. Each stage of the CODM process has specific tasks the facilitator must accomplish. These are described in Chapters 5

Facilitators can ensure greater responsiveness by periodically soliciting feedback from the group.

through 12. Throughout the entire process, however, the following primary duties need consistent attention.

Support Full Participation
- Encourage participation from all group members.
- Support group members when they make contributions.
- Help participants clarify and condense their ideas.
- Provide empathy to help group members feel understood.
- Ask for perspectives that have not yet been spoken.
- Ensure that no individuals dominate the discussion.
- Encourage group leaders to fully participate.

Support a Collaborative Atmosphere
- Inspire confidence in the potential for successful collaboration.
- Encourage egalitarian leadership (thinking about the whole group).
- Reframe judgments and criticisms.
- Help participants identify needs and underlying concerns.
- Interrupt disrespectful interactions.
- Identify common ground as it emerges.
- Challenge the group to work together to satisfy all relevant concerns.
- Guide the group to focus together on one idea at a time.
- Facilitate participants to listen and provide empathy to each other.

Manage the Flow of the Meeting
- Develop and manage the agenda based on the group goals and available time.
- Describe the overall design of the CODM process.
- Assign and supervise participants in any needed roles (timekeeper, chart scribe, minutes-taker).
- Explain the goals and activities involved in each step as the group progresses.
- Assess the needs of the group (break, empathy, contract for more time, progress to the next step, adjourn).

- Propose alternatives to adapt the process as needed by the group (shortcuts, small groups, go-rounds, delegating tasks to committees).
- Query the group for feedback about how the process is working.
- Apply the group's decision rule to finalize decisions about content or process.

These primary responsibilities serve to keep the group members all participating, working together and efficiently progressing toward a consensus-oriented decision. There are many communication skills that are useful in fulfilling these responsibilities. Several of these skills are described in the following chapters, particularly in the Communication Skill Builder sidebars. Additional training in communication skills is also helpful to any facilitator.

Final Decision Rules — What's Right for Your Group?

Before we can decide anything,
we must choose how our decisions will be made.

Any decision-making process will ultimately lead to the task of finalizing a decision. To finalize a decision, a group must use a final decision-making criterion (decision rule). A consensus-oriented process leads a group to solutions that generate as much agreement as possible. The decision rule, however, is what determines if the process has generated the degree of agreement necessary for a formal decision. The standard options are:[1]

- Person(s)-in-charge (a director or business owner decides)
- Executive committee (elected or appointed decision-making subgroup)
- Majority rule (votes determined by approval greater than 50%)
- Supermajority rule (votes determined by a high minimum percentage of approval)
- Unanimity (all group members must agree)

Groups benefit greatly from clearly choosing their final decision rule before they make a decision. Confusion about the decision process can undermine a group's ability to function well, especially in the final stages of a discussion. Unfortunately, some groups do not have a clear decision rule. In the midst of each discussion, they must generate both a proposal and a decision about what threshold of support is necessary for that proposal to be adopted. Establishing a clear decision rule, either formally (as in bylaws) or informally (as in everyone knows), allows the decision-making process to find an efficient conclusion.

A pre-established decision rule can be thought of as the default mechanism for finalizing decisions. Whenever there is confusion, the group can refer to its standard practice. Codifying the group's decision rule in writing can help eliminate any ambiguity. A written document (bylaws, operating agreement, charter, terms of employment) can also define specific conditions under which the group's decision rule may change. For instance, constitutional issues might require a supermajority for approval, whereas minor decisions may be decided by a simple majority. With this flexibility comes the need for a clear delineation of the different categories of decision that call for a different decision rule.

If the group chooses (using its default decision rule) it can temporarily change (raise or reduce) the standard for a particular decision. A majority rule group can decide, for instance, to require unanimity to enact a particularly important decision. Or a group that practices unanimity might all agree to allow the majority to rule on a particularly time-sensitive issue. Whenever the temporary decision to alter the decision rule expires or is challenged, the default decision rule returns as the basis for further decision-making.

Clearly choosing your group's decision rule is an important step in making your group function effectively. There are many variables to consider. The following discussion can help you decide what decision rule might suit your group to use as a default. If your group already has a clear decision rule, this discussion might help you decide if you might benefit from changing it.

If you are facilitating a group that you are not a member of, one of your first tasks is to assess the group's final decision rule. Is the rule clear? Is it documented? Is it accepted by everyone in the group? If not, there may be some active or underground power struggles in the group. If this dynamic is not dealt with up front, it may emerge in the midst of a discussion. Sometimes groups hire outside facilitators because this very problem has disrupted their decision-making capabilities. An outside facilitator can provide lasting assistance to a group by helping them clarify their decision rule before they try to make decisions.

Ms. Denton, a fourth-grade teacher, convened a meeting of all ten teachers in her school who shared responsibility for overseeing the children at recess periods. She told the group that she was concerned about some of the activities that occurred during recess. While she knew that there was no official policy on activities, she hoped the group could come up with some guidelines. She suggested that they discuss the issue and then take a vote.

In particular, Ms. Denton was concerned that dodgeball games during recess were being played with a level of aggression that she felt was frightening some of the children. She was also concerned about bullying behavior that she thought was associated with dodgeball. The group discussion went well, with most teachers in agreement that playing dodgeball should probably not be allowed.

At the close of the meeting, Ms. Denton asked, "So the proposal is that we do not allow dodgeball games anymore. Do we have a majority? How many say 'yes'?" At this request to finalize the decision, Mr. Fletcher, a sixth-grade teacher, spoke for the first time. "You all can do whatever you want. But I played dodgeball as a kid, and I decide what the kids do when I'm supervising them." Apparently the ad hoc group did not have a clearly accepted decision rule.

Person-in-Charge/Executive Committee

Everyone is very familiar with groups that are run by a particular authority figure in charge of decisions. This authority may reside in a single person or in a small group, such a board of directors. For simplicity, this discussion will refer to single person authority figures. When this authority rests in an executive committee, most of the same dynamics apply between those who hold the authority and the rest of the group members.

The authority to make decisions may be derived in different ways. It may be officially bestowed, such as through democratic election or business ownership. Or it may be established unofficially by factors such as age, experience or a dominant personality. Regardless of how the authority is granted, a group whose decisions are made by a person-in-charge or executive committee will function best if the decision-making authority is recognized and accepted by everyone in the group.

There are several advantages of person-in-charge decision-making. Of all the options, this method offers the greatest speed and efficiency. Further, if the person-in-charge is particularly skilled or has special expertise, she may make decisions that are more likely to succeed than a majority or supermajority decision of a group of people poorly educated on the topic. Finally, if the person-in-charge has made a substantially greater investment in the resources of the group (in time, money or material), the power to finalize decisions may be recognized as just and appropriate.

There are also well-known dangers to person-in-charge decision-making. Group members may not experience the autonomy or sense of equality they need when they do not have a share in the decision-making power. When these needs go badly unmet, people can be apathetic, passive-aggressive, defiant or openly rebellious. Collaborative decision-making in these circumstances is impaired by a lack of interest and/or trust and a dynamic of adversarial struggle.

Alternatively, group members may respond to the person-in-charge by aligning with the power of their authority. They may act compliant and ingratiating. Independent thinking, which might otherwise contribute to group decision-making, may be suppressed. This is especially likely if expressing personal perspectives risks generating conflict with the person-in-charge. People adopting a compliant strategy often find themselves in conflict, however, with fellow group members who have defiant or rebellious responses to authority.

Authority figures may have methods for securing cooperative behavior from the group. They may use rewards, such as a paycheck, or the threat of punishment to shape the behavior of the group. The full spirit of cooperation, however, is often less engaged than when group members feel they have a share of the power to make the decisions that affect them. Implementation of decisions that were not made inclusively can suffer. A lack of motivation, a passive response to emerging problems, blind obedience to obviously poor policies or outright sabotage are all potential dangers.

Person-in-charge decision-making places a great deal of responsibility on a single person (or small subgroup). The group depends on the person-in-charge to operate maturely and skillfully. This decision rule works best, therefore, when the person-in-charge has the personal maturity and training to operate effectively in the role. Otherwise, the drawbacks to this system become quite pronounced. Much of the dissatisfaction of workers in hierarchical settings can be traced to the drawbacks of person-in-charge decision-making. When this authority is poorly wielded, the atmosphere and functionality of an entire organization can suffer terribly. The resulting misery is one of the primary problems Consensus-Oriented Decision-Making seeks to address.

The group is also best served when the person-in-charge can understand all the multiple perspectives of the different stakeholders in a decision. This is impossible without considerable communication. Isolated leaders are unlikely to make effective decisions. The difficulty of gathering multiple perspectives is increased as the size of a group increases. In large groups, leaders will need some organized means of gathering input from group members. This can be done through staging large membership meetings, through convening meetings with representatives from the various sections of the larger membership or through using appropriate virtual (computer) communication tools.

Using CODM with a Person-in-Charge Decision Rule

Consensus-Oriented Decision-Making offers a chance for authority decision makers to include the whole group's input. Doing so can tap the group's cumulative intelligence and creativity. It can also inspire a greater spirit of cooperation by meeting the group members' needs for inclusion in and ownership of important decisions.

There are some very important considerations, however, when a person-in-charge offers to engage a group in a CODM process. First, it is vital that the issue and terms of the discussion be clearly framed. What is the issue the person-in-charge wants discussed? Why is this issue being offered to the group? How will the final decision maker treat the proposal the group produces? The goal of this framing is to help the group understand the boundaries of any decision-making power they are being offered. Any misunderstanding about this could be very problematic.

A person-in-charge must demonstrate respect for any input they receive from the group. Otherwise, any future attempt to engage the group in a CODM process may be undermined. The group's primary motivation for engaging in the challenge of collaborative decision-making is the hope that the result will be fruitful. It is not very motivating to create a proposal that is then discarded. Thus, the person-in-charge must make it clear that the group's work is valued. The most direct way to do this is for the person-in-charge to adopt the group's proposal as a final decision.

If the group's proposal is not adopted, for any reason, the person-in-charge can still show respect for the group. Communicating the ways that the group's proposal influenced the final result can help the group members feel valued. Explaining what factors contributed to a decision that differed from the group's proposal is also important. If a person-in-charge wants the group to help with decision-making in the future, he should make sure the group knows that their work was truly appreciated, even if it was not adopted.

Ultimately, a group will want to see at least a portion of its input or decisions adopted. The value of a rich and motivated group decision-making process is often more important than any particular decision. Even if an authority figure believes she has a slightly better idea, it may be best to yield to the group's proposal. The shared ownership of a group decision can foster considerable commitment to the successful implementation of group-generated proposals. A "B grade" decision executed well because of a strong sense of shared ownership may have far better results than an "A grade" decision poorly implemented because of lackluster support.

Majority Rule

Majority rule is also a very familiar decision rule. In majority rule, proposals that receive more than 50% of the vote are adopted. Usually votes are allotted an equal ratio of one vote per person. Sometimes, however, there is a reason to weigh some people's votes more than others (for instance, votes may be distributed in proportion to how much ownership stake each participant has in a business).

There are several advantages in using majority rule. It provides an easily understood way to make decisions efficiently. It can be applied in almost all circumstances (except when there is not a sufficient quorum present). It works in large or small groups. It allows all members of a group to participate and register a vote. And the process of majority voting is generally considered to be just and valid (assuming the absence of fraud) even if the results are disappointing or objectionable to the losing parties.

The primary drawbacks to majority rule, however, are worth careful consideration.

First, the very quickness and efficiency with which a vote can be taken makes majority rule susceptible to poorly considered decisions. If a particular faction of a group captures a majority of the group's membership, they can generate a proposal and pass it without including any of the perspective, creativity or wisdom of the minority members of the group. This exclusion can make the decisions generated less well considered. They may overlook certain points of view entirely. It can also make implementation of the decisions vulnerable to sabotage from a defiant minority who feel shut out of the process.

Second, the politics of generating a majority can undermine group cohesion. Members may form factions to protect themselves from being isolated and overwhelmed by other factions in the group. The merits of any particular proposal may become secondary to the importance of maintaining cohesion within a faction. A group member may cast votes according to his subgroup affiliations, rather than according to his conscience or best judgment. The best outcome for the group as a whole becomes secondary to the power struggle for control of the group.

Third, majority rule allows what might be a temporary mood of a group to easily change an established status quo. This makes the group's decisions more vulnerable to immediately attractive but poorly considered ideas. It also makes a group susceptible to repeatedly reversing its decisions, especially when it is almost evenly split on an issue.

These drawbacks can be addressed by utilizing a decision-making process that ensures inclusive, collaborative and thoughtful consideration of any proposal before making a decision. Combining a consensus-oriented process, like CODM, with an efficient final decision-making process, like majority rule, can maximize the two goals of participation and efficiency. The success of this combination, however, depends upon a group's willingness to commit to the spirit of a consensus-oriented process. Otherwise, the drawbacks of majority rule may not be adequately avoided.

Supermajority Rule

Supermajority rule requires a larger percentage of agreement than majority rule.

Supermajority rule requires a larger percentage of agreement than majority rule. A supermajority threshold can theoretically be anything between simple majority and unanimity. Common figures include 60%, 65%, two-thirds and 75%. Some groups have chosen to mitigate the problems of required unanimity by choosing a supermajority threshold of 80%, 90%, "unanimity minus one" or "unanimity minus two." Democratic organizations and governments often employ supermajority as the decision rule for structural changes to an established system, like amendments to a nation's constitution.

As a decision rule, supermajority can be a satisfying compromise. It can offer protection from the potential drawbacks of majority rule. Decisions made by supermajority require greater agreement than simple majority votes. Thus, the process to reach a supermajority decision must include more of the group. A majority faction cannot function without reaching out and working with its opposition. The requirement of greater participation ensures that more of the group has a voice. It also protects the status quo from change based on the temporary or controversial whim of a simple majority.

A supermajority decision rule can also be applied specifically to the issue of closing debate. For instance, the US Senate requires a 60% supermajority to close debate on legislation. This raises the threshold of agreement necessary. Controversial issues that would pass a majority vote cannot succeed without a supermajority agreeing to bring the issue to a vote.

Supermajority can also be a valuable alternative to mitigate the problems associated with required unanimity. A high supermajority threshold can force a group to use a highly participatory process, while still providing a way to make a decision without complete unanimity. This can prevent the widespread dissatisfaction that can occur if one or two people succeed in blocking an otherwise unanimous decision.

Supermajority, unfortunately, retains some of the pitfalls of both simple majority and required unanimity. It remains possible for a sufficiently large faction of a group to ignore the participation of a small minority. This leaves the group vulnerable to missing a vital perspective on an issue, especially when only one or two people hold that perspective. A group with a supermajority threshold is also vulnerable to widespread disagreement when the threshold is almost, but not quite reached. In this case a minority of the group prevails in blocking a decision. Supermajority thresholds prevent this minority from being as small as one person, but rule by a minority of any size can generate problems in a group. This is sometimes referred to as the *tyranny of the minority*. A sense of frustration and injustice is likely within any majority subgroup whose proposal has been defeated.

Unanimity

Some groups that strongly value participatory decision-making use unanimity as the standard for finalizing a decision. Unless everyone agrees, no decision moves forward. This decision rule forces groups to be very participatory. And when unanimity is achieved, the group benefits greatly from having all members on board. This decision rule is particularly indicated when a group cannot afford to lose a participant. The permanent members of the United Nations Security Council, for instance, use this decision rule because of the danger that if any of the world's major military powers leaves the group, because it objects to a decision, the prospect of war is increased.

Unanimity and Consensus

As discussed in Chapter 1, the terms *unanimity* and *consensus* are often used interchangeably. This book uses separate meanings for these words. *Unanimity* refers to a final decision rule that requires full agreement for a decision to be made. *Consensus* refers to the fully participatory process a group may use to develop proposals. A consensus process can be used in conjunction with any final decision rule.

Requiring unanimity for a decision forces a group to use a participatory, consensus-oriented process. All the benefits of this type of process are thus ensured, if the group succeeds in reaching full agreement. Large factions in the group cannot exert their will over other group members. Each person's concerns must be incorporated into the decision sufficiently to gain everyone's support. This guaranteed inclusion of all perspectives helps participants feel confident throughout the discussion that nothing they disagree with will be approved by the group.

Unfortunately, no consensus process can ever ensure unanimous approval of the resulting proposal. Groups that have unanimity as a decision rule are sometimes troubled, therefore, when they do not achieve it. Lacking an alternative way to finalize a decision, such groups may flounder, be ruled by a minority of dissenters or remain stuck with the status quo. These dynamics are discussed more thoroughly in Chapter 12, which looks in depth at the dynamics of groups that require unanimity.

To remedy the problems encountered when a group cannot reach unanimity, various adaptations to this decision rule have been employed. Often, the definition of support for a proposal is softened by asking, "Is this proposal something you can live with?" This framing of the question makes unanimity easier to reach because the goal is full "consent" rather than full "agreement." Some groups have a fallback decision rule that allows for a supermajority to finalize a decision when unanimity fails. Other groups delegate decision-making to a committee when the whole group becomes stuck. Often, groups use unanimity for a decision rule only on major decisions affecting the fundamental values of the group. For more routine decisions, a more efficient decision rule is applied. These adaptations can help make unanimity a more effective decision rule.

CODM is a process that seeks to generate as much agreement as possible. CODM is, therefore, a valuable way for a group to try to satisfy a decision rule of unanimity. While unanimous consent can never be guaranteed, a consensus-oriented process is the best way to attempt it. Requiring unanimity is one way to try to ensure that a group will use a participatory process. It can be effective, as long as there is a good plan for what to do if full agreement is not possible.

In 1980 a group of men, influenced by feminism, formed a collective to run a counseling agency to treat male batterers. They made decisions by unanimous consent at monthly meetings of members of the collective. The agency became quite successful, and after a few years in business, it started to hire staff to run its anti-violence groups. The hired counselors were primarily interns from graduate counseling programs at nearby universities.

Several staff counselors were eager to offer couple counseling to some of the agency clients. The collective opposed this idea because they believed the practice might run counter to the feminist message that men must take full responsibility for violence against women. Eventually, however, most of the collective was persuaded to allow couple counseling at the agency. Two collective members, however, remained opposed, and they blocked any decision to reverse the established policy. The strength of their political convictions was immovable.

Some staff counselors decided that they were more determined to serve their clients than they were bound to the dictates of the collective. They began to schedule couple counseling sessions at the agency in the evenings, when the practice would not likely be observed. Not surprisingly, this activity was eventually discovered, and a crisis at the agency erupted. Half the counseling staff faced being fired for insubordination.

A mediator was consulted and interviewed the various participants. He concluded that the agency suffered from the worst of two different decision-making criteria. Within the collective, the members were unable to update their policies, despite a widespread desire to do so. The unanimity rule had generated enormous frustration within the collective members. Some were threatening to leave. Others threatened to kick out the two who blocked change.

Meanwhile, the staff counselors suffered from the autocratic rule they experienced in relation to the collective. Their participation was not included at meetings of the collective. So while the collective tried very hard to reach agreement among themselves, they did not give a voice to the staff in their meetings. Consequently, the staff had little investment in following the rules handed down to them.

The mediator succeeded in convincing the whole agency that the problem was not in any of the specific people. Rather, the problem lay in the system of decision-making the agency used. A meeting of the whole agency was called. The mediator facilitated a group agreement to redesign its decision-making process. Unanimity was dropped as the decision rule, in favor of a 65% supermajority criterion. Staff counselors were invited to participate in collective meetings. A committee was formed to define the protocol under which couple counseling would be allowed. No one was fired. One of the founding collective members resigned in opposition to the changes. The other stayed, continuing to make sure feminist perspectives were included in future decisions.

What Will Work Best for Your Group?

Each group is unique. So there is no universally correct choice for the proper final decision rule. There are many variables to consider. The following chart summarizes much of the information in this chapter by analyzing how different variables are affected in the four different types of decision rules. Whatever choice your group makes, it will benefit from having that choice clear to all members of the group.

One thing all the options have in common is that they can each employ CODM as a process. The group's decision rule does not determine the process used for generating proposals. CODM can help any group generate proposals with full participation in an efficient stepwise procedure. Then, depending on the group, any final decision rule can be used to adopt or reject the proposal. Using CODM can help all groups reap the benefits of generating as much agreement as possible.

FIGURE 3.1. Comparing Final Decision Rules

Variable	Person-in-Charge	Majority	Supermajority	Required Unanimity
Level of Agreement	Varies, depending on the leader's efforts to generate group agreement through a participatory process.	Theoretically at least, a majority agree to any decision. There may be substantial disagreement among the minority. And faction members may vote according to their political allegiance rather than their true preference.	When supermajority is not quite reached, there may be more than half the group in disagreement with the result.	When unanimity is reached, agreement is full. When unanimity is not reached, widespread disagreement may prevail.
Size of Group	The smaller the group, the easier it is for one person to assess the needs of the whole group.	Works for small or large groups. May not work for very small groups (under seven members).	Works for small or large groups. May not work for very small groups (under seven members).	The smaller the group, the less chance of blocked decisions.
Time Commitment	Leader must devote time to decisions. The group need not.	Group needs to devote enough time to make an informed choice.	Group needs to devote enough time to make an informed choice.	Group members must devote a lot of time to process decisions together.

Variable	Person-in-Charge	Majority	Supermajority	Required Unanimity
Importance of Relationships	Flexible. Depends on leader's style.	Attention to relationships is not required. If factions develop, however, relationships can become political and require attention.	Attention to relationships is not required.	Group members must be committed to processing relationship issues.
Training	Leader must be highly trained.	Group members do not need special training.	Group members do not need special training.	Group must be highly trained.
Maturity	Leader must function well.	People of all maturity levels can participate.	People of all maturity levels can participate.	All group members must function well.
Protection of Status Quo	Status quo can be quickly and arbitrarily changed.	Status quo is vulnerable to change.	Status quo is well protected.	Status quo is very strongly protected.
Vulnerability to a Non-Inclusive Process	Vulnerable to ignoring many perspectives.	Vulnerable to ignoring minority perspectives.	Ensures inclusion of more perspectives.	Ensures inclusion of all perspectives.
Efficiency	Highest efficiency.	High efficiency.	Can be efficient, unless stalemates prevent the group from reaching a decision.	More time may be spent making decisions. But implementing decisions may be very smooth.
Perception of Justice	Varies greatly, from a sense of chronic injustice to acceptance and gratefulness for quality leadership.	Generally accepted as just, unless political manipulations were employed.	When a popular proposal does not quite reach the supermajority threshold, a sense of injustice may be felt.	Whenever unanimity is not quite reached, a distinct sense of injustice may prevail.
Open Membership	Accommodates open membership, if all members respect the leadership.	Accommodates open membership.	Accommodates open membership.	Works best with carefully selected membership, and in closed groups where all members have strong relationships.
Group Cohesion	Varies from disconnected to team oriented, depending on leadership.	Varies. Can be prone to competing factions.	Varies.	Very strong when successful. Vulnerable to schism when unanimity fails.

CODM Process
Overview—
The Seven Steps

This chapter offers an overview of the seven steps in the CODM process. It shows how the steps systematically lead a group toward a decision. Each individual step is more fully explained in the following chapters. If you want to use CODM effectively in your group, be sure to read the whole book. The details of each step are important to understand well. Once you have read the whole book, however, reviewing this chapter will help you conceptualize the entire process more easily.

An Outline of the Steps

The basic components of the CODM process are summarized below:

- **Step 1:** Framing the Topic. The facilitator prepares for the meeting, ensuring that the group has the right context, structure and information it may need for a successful discussion.
- **Step 2:** Open Discussion. The facilitator structures a discussion to allow a creative mix of divergent viewpoints.
- **Step 3:** Identifying Underlying Concerns. All stakeholders affected by a decision are identified. The concerns of each of these parties are considered and added to the mix.

- **Step 4:** Collaborative Proposal Development. Selected ideas are developed into proposal options, one at a time. The whole group tries to build each option so that it addresses all the identified concerns as much as possible.
- **Step 5:** Choosing a Direction. The group analyzes support for the options and selects one to develop further.
- **Step 6:** Synthesizing a Final Proposal. The chosen proposal is amended to maximize its potential to address all concerns and gain support from the group.
- **Step 7:** Closure. The group finalizes its decision and, optionally, addresses any remaining concerns about the process.

This full seven-step process is especially useful for complex decisions that would benefit from a maximum level of group participation. Routine decisions, however, are not likely to require the group to progress through all seven steps. To accommodate different situations and different types of decisions, the CODM process can be modified in a number of ways. Shortcuts to the process can reduce the time it takes for a group to reach a decision. Several common shortcuts are illustrated at the end of this chapter. If the full process seems too cumbersome for a particular decision, one of these shortcuts is probably indicated.

Step 1: Frame the Topic

Framing a topic is the task of preparing the context in which the topic will be discussed. The facilitator frames a topic, like a picture frame around an artwork, by considering how an issue can best be placed before the group. What are the goals of the discussion? Who should be present? What information might the group need? How should the discussion be structured? These are some of the questions that need to be considered before the group even meets. This preparation helps ensure the group process will be efficient.

Each topic of group discussion begins with someone suggesting a problem (or an idea) they think the group should address. Often this takes the form of asking to have a topic placed on the group's agenda. The facilitator then discusses the topic with the person presenting it. What do they know about this topic? What are their goals for the discussion? The discussion can be formal or informal. To get additional points of view, the facilitator can also speak to other group members about the topic. Here are some examples of questions that can help generate a thoughtful framing of an issue prior to opening up a group discussion:

- Is the presenter identifying a perceived problem, a proposed solution or both?
- Who is likely to have an interest in this topic?
- Is this group the appropriate body to discuss this topic?
- Is the topic something the group needs to make a decision about?
- What priority is this topic for the group?
- How much time might the group want to devote to this topic?
- What information might the group need to meaningfully discuss the issue?
- What interpersonal dynamics might affect the discussion?

Once an agenda item has been carefully considered, the facilitator can plan how to structure the discussion. The facilitator can assess how much time to devote to the topic and what priority it may have on the agenda. Should the full CODM process be used, or would a shortcut be more appropriate? The facilitator can also work with the participants presenting the topic to formulate the best way to open the discussion. The following example points out the value of carefully framing a topic, rather than just placing items on an agenda.

A blank paper was posted on the bulletin board in the lunchroom at a weekly newspaper office. At the top, Jean, the office manager, had written "Meeting Agenda." One of the items soon listed by Chip, from the ad sales team, read "Proper diet." Kate, a graphic designer with an eating disorder, got scared. She did not want Chip lecturing the group about how to eat. The topic was too sensitive for her. She demanded that Jean take it off the agenda, saying that, otherwise, she would not be able to attend the meeting.

Instead, Jean approached Chip and asked him what the item meant to him and what he hoped to accomplish with a group discussion. It turned out that Chip was only trying to change the content of the lunchroom vending machines. He did not want to be constantly tempted by the junk food they offered. Having identified the real issue, Jean reframed the agenda item and listed it as "Vending machine contents." Kate was much relieved and became an ally for Chip in the ensuing discussion.

Step 2: Open Discussion

After a topic has been presented to the group, the CODM process calls for an open discussion of the issue. Within an appropriate, simple structure, group members are encouraged to identify different ways of seeing the problem (some might not see a problem at all) and different ideas for solutions. If the discussion is open and supportive, the facilitator may allow it to continue with minimal structure. If the discussion becomes competitive or judgmental, the facilitator can guide the group by adding more structure to the session. Different ways of structuring open discussion, such as brainstorming, go-arounds and facilitator-centered discussion techniques, are described in Chapter 6.

The purpose of this step is to generate a wide range of possibilities for the group to consider. Even ideas at the outer edge of what a majority might consider reasonable are important contributions at this stage of the process. They help group members think outside the box and enhance a sense of creativity. Each idea, no matter how outrageous, does contain some genius. It usually addresses a particular aspect of the problem in a way that might be worth considering, if only to increase awareness of an otherwise poorly recognized piece of the whole puzzle.

A group of seniors operating a nonprofit thrift store met to discuss how they would staff the store over the summer, when many of them hoped to travel out of the area. Nancy shocked the group by suggesting that they "just close the store and all get on with their lives." While no one actually wanted to do this, her suggestion helped them all realize the degree to which they were feeling burned out. This awareness eventually led them to prioritize bringing new members into the group.

Open discussion is a vital part of the CODM process. If it is rushed, then the group moves on to narrow its options without having creatively identified a wide range of possibilities. The facilitator can keep the discussion enjoyable by enthusiastically supporting all suggestions. Providing positive reinforcement for outrageous ideas can be very fun and can help the group relax in preparation for working together in the following steps.

Step 3: Identify Underlying Concerns

In this step, the facilitator asks the group to focus attention on the underlying needs and concerns that are affected by the issue being discussed. Often people think in terms of solutions, without clearly identifying the needs those solutions are intended to meet. When disagreement arises, parties can quickly begin defending their positions on what solution will work best. A polarized and contentious argument is often the result. Thus, the importance of identifying underlying needs and concerns cannot be overstated.

When all of the underlying concerns are identified, the groundwork is laid for collaborating to find more comprehensive solutions. Instead of debating whether to choose between plan X that meets need X or plan Y that meets need Y, the group can work together on a new plan that meets all needs (X and Y) as much as possible.

The facilitator begins by asking the group to identify all stakeholders that may be affected by a decision on the topic. It is particularly important to identify any stakeholders that may not be represented in the group. Then, the group is asked to list all the needs and concerns each stakeholder may have. Different group members may champion different needs as they are expressed. But in the end, the whole group is asked to metaphorically put all the concerns listed into the same basket. Instead of considering only the concerns with which they identify, each group member is asked to try to come up with solutions that meet all the concerns in the common basket.

A family came to a mediator to resolve a power struggle between the parents and their teenage daughter, Joni. The parents were making plans to take the daughter and her younger siblings on vacation. Joni, however, refused to go on another "boring" family trip. The parents put their feet down and insisted she come. Joni, in return, refused to come to the dinner table, infuriating the parents. In the mediator's office, Joni demanded that the family go on vacation without her. The parents demanded that Joni "suck it up" and come.

When the mediator asked what underlying needs were at play, the discussion opened up. Joni expressed a need for peer contact and relief from the annoying behavior of her younger brother, Jimmy. The parents expressed a need to stay connected to Joni in a way that their daily schedules did not allow. When the mediator asked for ideas about how all these needs could be met, some new ideas began to surface. Eventually the parents altered the vacation plans so that the trip could include a friend of Joni's, and they planned activities that would occupy Jimmy well. Joni then acknowledged the value of vacationing as a family, and she agreed to go.

Step 4: Collaborative Proposal Development

Once all the underlying needs and concerns have been listed, the group is ready to begin collaborating on how to satisfy those concerns through various proposals. Without facilitation, this discussion often becomes competitive. Group members may begin arguing about the value of one proposal over another. In the CODM process, this contentious approach is avoided by giving each proposal a turn to be developed to its full potential by the whole group.

Collaborating to develop proposals is similar to the way settlers on the North American frontier would cooperate to help each other build their barns. Building a barn was too big a job for one family. But three families could raise three barns, if they all worked together.

As simple as this concept sounds, it may be profoundly different from the way many people are accustomed to approaching group discussions. Adopting a collaborative approach may represent a quantum change in consciousness or mindset. Some group members may have difficulty understanding this new approach. They may not know how to drop their familiar style of competitive and adversarial debate. The facilitator can help by clearly describing the process and intervening whenever collaboration is being undermined. The group members benefit not only from building solutions together, but from experiencing a new way of working together.

In this step, each different idea becomes a starting point for building a solution that satisfies all the concerns at issue. If there are four competing approaches, each one gets a turn. During that turn, the whole group is asked to develop the idea into the best solution it can be. Even group members who are adverse to the idea are asked to contribute suggestions for improving it. The turn proceeds until the group has exhausted its creative possibilities for that idea. Then, a different idea is offered a turn as the starting point. The group then builds upon that idea in a similar fashion. At all times, the whole group is working together on the same idea, building each one out as well as it can.

Step 5: Choose a Direction

After a productive barn-building session, the group will be equipped to move into a decision-making phase. All the favorable proposal ideas will have been explored, and their potential as solutions will have been well discussed. In this step, the facilitator leads the group in a comparative analysis of the pros and cons of each of the resulting options. Following this, the group chooses which of the possible directions to pursue. This choice is a defining moment, a significant movement toward decision.

In this step, the group does not decide on a final proposal. But it does choose what direction that final proposal will take. A *preference gradient* voting process (see Chapter 9) is used. Participants are able to register the degree to which they support an idea, with more than just a yes or no vote. This allows the group to gauge the degree of ambivalence that may be present. And it helps determine if there is a clear choice. After this vote, the group will continue to refine the solution it is developing. The continued input of participants who still have reservations is essential to the success of subsequent stages of the process.

Step 6: Synthesize a Final Proposal

Once a direction is chosen, the group can begin synthesizing a comprehensive final proposal. The goal of this stage is to collaboratively develop a single proposal so that it maximally satisfies all the needs and concerns the group has identified. Much of this work may have been done in Step 4. But once a particular direction is actually chosen, a second effort is useful. Anyone who may have held back during the option development step will have another chance to make sure their concerns are incorporated into the final proposal. Alternatively, this step can be delegated to a subcommittee. This shortcut is advised whenever the patience of the whole group would be taxed by deciding relatively unimportant details of the final proposal.

This step begins with a formal listening session. Anyone who sees needs or concerns that are not addressed sufficiently by the chosen direction has a chance to articulate their perspective. In response, the facilitator or other group members use reflective listening to convey an understanding of whatever is being expressed. This process helps all participants feel heard. It also ensures that the group accurately understands the concerns being expressed.

Once the unaddressed needs and concerns are understood, the proposal is amended in any way that will improve it. Often, ideas floated earlier are adopted. Sometimes, however, new ideas arise in the midst of this step. The popularity of any amendment can be easily assessed with a straw poll, using a preference gradient voting process. Ideas that make the proposal more broadly accepted are particularly sought. Expanding the extent to which the proposal meets all the underlying needs and concerns is the main goal. At the conclusion of this process, the group can develop the formal wording of the resulting proposal. This sets the stage for closure on a formal decision.

Step 7: Closure

Once the final proposal is settled, the group's decision rule can be formally applied. If the group rules require unanimity, supermajority or simple majority, a vote can be taken. Then, the facilitator announces whether the necessary threshold of approval has been reached. If a person-in-charge (or governing committee) has final decision-making authority, the facilitator asks that person (or committee) if she is ready to decide.

The group's work is not necessarily over with a decision, however. There are several optional substeps that can enhance a sense of closure to the process. The first of these is to provide empathy to anyone who is not satisfied with the result. Despite a group's best effort, the final decision may not meet all the needs and concerns that were expressed. Participants who still have concerns may benefit from receiving empathy for any feelings they may have about the outcome. This is not the time to reopen the possibility of changing the group's decision. Rather, it is a time to express understanding and caring to whatever emotions participants may have about either the process or the resulting decision. Often, if they receive empathy, participants can move through their feelings and begin to embrace the will of the group.

The CODM process can be modified to serve a variety of different circumstances.

Another optional step of closure is a request for cooperation in implementing the decision. This request can come from the facilitator or any other group member. Verbalizing this request makes explicit the hope that everyone will respect the decision and not undermine its successful application. No one's cooperation can be secured by this request. But verbalizing it can raise the consciousness of each participant to consider their own choices about how they will respond to this decision and whether they will cooperate or not with the decision the group has made.

Modifying CODM

The CODM process can be modified to serve a variety of different circumstances. Decisions that are very important to the group, such as long-term planning, structural/organizational change or resolution of a group crisis, are likely to benefit from use of the full process. Routine decisions, time-sensitive decisions or decisions that impact only part of a group, however, may be better served by a simpler structure that takes less group time. Often, there is a balance to strike between maximizing group participation versus minimizing the time spent in group discussions. The main way to save the whole group's time is to delegate different steps in the process to individuals or committees. This work can be more time efficient, but it does result in less participation of the whole group. Depending on the topic, the facilitator can help the group decide which steps should include the whole group and which steps can be delegated to a committee.

CODM Shortcuts

The following shortcuts are common adaptations that can help groups reduce the time they spend meeting, while retaining the level of participation they choose. The options are depicted in flowcharts, progressing from the full CODM process to the quickest possible version. In the flowcharts, circles are used for steps the whole group participates in and rectangles are used for steps delegated to individuals or committees. In addition to these options, each group or facilitator can create their own custom adaptations. Being familiar with how the process can be modified can help a facilitator suggest changes whenever they would be useful.

FIGURE 4.1. Full CODM Process

Final Proposal Committee Shortcut

In this shortcut, the task of working out the details of the final proposal is delegated to a committee. This is most appropriate when the whole group is primarily concerned with only the basic direction of a decision. Often there are particular group members with certain expertise for deciding details that do not need the whole group's attention. In this shortcut, the group may be able to experience closure to the issue, trusting the committee to finish the job. Alternatively the whole group could ask the final proposal committee to report back to the whole group for closure to the process. The use of a final proposal committee can be combined with any of the following options as well.

FIGURE 4.2. Final Proposal Committee Shortcut

Preparation Committee Shortcut

A preparation committee (or individual) can save the group time by identifying stakeholders and their underlying concerns in advance of the meeting. The group can add to this list if any additional stakeholders or concerns are identified in the open discussion.

FIGURE 4.3. Preparation Committee Shortcut

Proposal Presentation Committee Shortcut

In this shortcut, a committee prepares the topic by completing Steps 1, 2 and 3. It then presents several proposal options for the group to review in open discussion. Each of the options should be designed to satisfy the identified concerns as much as possible. The group discussion can then review the committee work, supplying additional creativity and correcting any errors or omissions. Diligent committee work in presenting proposals can significantly reduce the need for group discussion time. Delegating this degree of preparation to a committee, however, does reduce the group's participation in the early stages of conceptualizing the topic.

FIGURE 4.4. Proposal Presentation Committee Shortcut

Proposal Development Committee Shortcut

This shortcut requires two meetings. In between the meetings, a committee takes the conceptual framework of the topic developed in the group discussion and uses it to develop specific proposal options to be presented to the group. The group then chooses one option to develop into a final proposal. This allows the group to participate in conceiving the topic and identifying the concerns that need to be addressed. The group saves time, however, by delegating the task of generating the proposal options. When special expertise is needed to develop complex proposals, this modification of the process is indicated. It allows experts to receive input from the group prior to proposal development and then allows the group to fully deliberate the resulting proposal.

FIGURE 4.5. Proposal Development Committee Shortcut

Routine Decision Shortcut

For routine decisions, a streamlined process is most appropriate. The benefits of a consensus-oriented process are generally dwarfed by the need for an efficient method of moving through agenda items that are less significant. The basic pattern follows a very familiar and intuitive sequence:

- What is the problem?
- What are the alternatives for addressing it?
- Which alternative do we choose?
- Who is going to figure out the details?

FIGURE 4.6. Routine Decision Shortcut

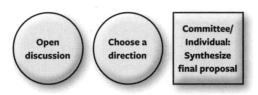

In general, routine decisions do not require a facilitator to prepare the group by framing the topic. The topic might not even enter the agenda until after the start of a meeting. The facilitator does have an important role, however, in maintaining a cooperative atmosphere during the discussion. And the facilitator can assist the group's efficiency in several ways:

- Summarizing any concerns or proposals that have been raised
- Identifying when a topic is not routine and deserves a more thoughtful process
- Identifying when the group is ready to make a decision
- Applying the group's decision rule
- Clarifying who is taking responsibility for the next steps or action items

Spontaneous Resolution

Sometimes a group will discover a solution that gains widespread support in the midst of one of any CODM steps. It is vital that the facilitator recognize this when it occurs. There is no point in continuing through a stepwise model when a group has spontaneously solved its problem already. When success arises, the group may be authentically ready to move on. If so, the facilitator can articulate this possibility to the group for confirmation. Then, the process can advance to any needed aspects of closure. The

FIGURE 4.7. Spontaneous Resolution Flowchart

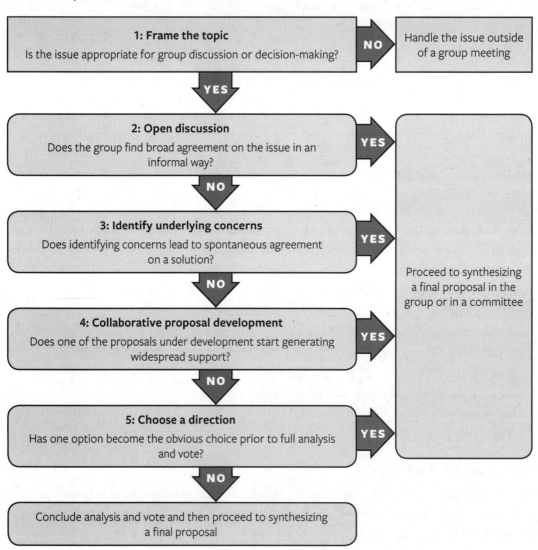

following flowchart depicts how spontaneous resolution may occur at any stage of the process.

Spontaneous resolution should be carefully assessed. Sometimes a group may present a "head nod" agreement that is not authentic. Power dynamics, impatience or a lack of confidence that true collaboration is possible may all result in superficial approval of an idea that is not actually popular. This can be very unhealthy for a group. Implementation of such decisions may be undermined by passive or active resistance later on. The facilitator should be aware of this danger. She can test the group's sincerity by directly asking about the true level of support participants are feeling for a particular idea. If significant dissension is unearthed, the facilitator can advise the group to consider carefully whether to proceed with a more thorough process or skip to a more expedient closure.

Summary

The CODM process, in its full seven-step format, offers a very effective way to lead a group through a participatory decision-making process. The process can be modified with the shortcuts above, or other variations your group might choose, to balance the need for time efficiency with the benefits of a fully participatory process. This chapter has provided an overview of the process. A detailed understanding of the steps, however, is very important for a facilitator to use CODM effectively. Thus, each of the steps is described more thoroughly in the following chapters. When you are ready to use CODM, a single-page outline of the steps is available in the appendix for use as a crib sheet.

The CODM process, in its full seven-step format, offers a very effective way to lead a group through a participatory decision-making process.

FIGURE 4.8. Summary of Key Ideas in the CODM Process

Decision Process vs. Decision Rule	A consensus-oriented process can help any group generate widespread agreement. It is the process that generates the agreement, not the decision rule a group uses. Groups can choose any type of decision rule to finalize their decisions once they have maximized agreement using a consensus-oriented process.
Stepwise Facilitation	The CODM steps help a group make consistent progress toward a decision. A description of the steps helps participants understand and trust the process. This allows the group to focus on the content of the issue while the facilitator guides the group through the steps. It prevents the frustration participants experience when they do not know where the discussion is headed.
Framing Issues Prior to Discussion	Understanding the dynamics of an issue and clarifying the goals for discussion prior to a meeting can help a group proceed efficiently. It can also identify and separate personal issues from whole group issues.
Safe Atmosphere	The inclusion, participation and creative contribution of all group members is enhanced by structures and facilitation that ensure a safe and supportive group atmosphere.
Identifying Underlying Needs	Prior to generating or discussing proposals, the group identifies the underlying needs of all stakeholders. This depolarizes any premature standoff between opposing positions. It establishes the criteria for a successful solution, and it sets the stage for collaborative solution building.
Collaboration Process	The group takes turns, working together to develop options that satisfy the underlying concerns of all stakeholders as much as possible. The competitiveness of polarizing debate is avoided, and the whole group contributes to the resulting decision.
Preference Gradient Voting vs. Yes or No Decision	When votes are taken, a preference gradient voting process reveals not just a verdict. It elicits more information about the level of support an idea enjoys. This helps a group better understand how to maximize agreement even further.
Group Relationship Building	The CODM process not only helps groups make decisions. It teaches groups how to build safe, supportive and collaborative relationships. Successful group decision-making fosters a positive group atmosphere, increases group cohesion and builds cooperation.

Step 1:
Framing the Issue

The first step of CODM begins before the group even meets. It's about preparation. It involves thinking through the essence of a group discussion topic. In this step, a facilitator researches both the intentions of the person raising the issue and the needs the group may have in addressing it. What are the goals for the discussion? How could CODM or a shortcut version of CODM assist? How can the discussion get a healthy start? This effort to carefully frame and clarify the issue provides the platform for the group to work upon.

1. Collect agenda items.
2. Clarify the essence, goals and appropriate process for each issue.
3. Interview a sample of group members.
4. Identify and delegate useful pre-meeting research.
5. Introduce the discussion.

Collect Agenda Items
A facilitator's first job is to collect group discussion topic suggestions. In some groups, the agenda items are selected by the group's leader. The

facilitator can review the topics simply by meeting with the person-in-charge and discussing the upcoming agenda. In other groups, any group member may submit an agenda item. In this case, the facilitator must choose how to collect agenda suggestions from the group. It is fairly common practice to call for agenda items at the beginning of a meeting. This method, however, does not give a facilitator a chance to prepare for the ensuing discussions. Generally, meetings run much more efficiently when an agenda is prepared before the meeting.

A facilitator's first job is to collect group discussion topic suggestions.

Agenda topic suggestions from group members may be submitted publicly or privately. Public methods include posting suggestions on a bulletin board (physical or electronic) or submitting suggestions to a group e-mail list. Often, public posting can work fine. Sometimes, however, public posting can become chaotic. The agenda can get too full, or some of the items may not be appropriate for one reason or another.

When a facilitator receives suggestions privately, she has more opportunity to screen questionable items before the group begins responding to them. To receive agenda items privately, the facilitator solicits each group member separately with a request for suggestions. This can be done in person, by phone or through individual e-mail. Alternatively, a group notice or e-mail can be posted with a request that replies be sent just to the facilitator.

Sometimes group members may suspect that a private submission process is an attempt at secrecy. This dynamic is more likely when trust levels in the group are low. The facilitator can address this concern by explaining the value of clarifying topic suggestions prior to group discussion. Reassurance can be offered that framing a topic for discussion helps the facilitator prepare a process to efficiently address the topic. It is not an attempt to skew or bias the outcome of any decision that the discussion may ultimately produce.

- "Please send your agenda items directly to me rather than posting them to the whole group. I'd like to have a chance to discuss the item with you prior to the meeting. That way I can make sure I fully understand it before placing it on the agenda."

- "If you want to put an item on the agenda, please call me first so we can talk about it. It helps me to know in advance what your goals for the group discussion might be."

Clarify the Issue

The central component of framing a topic for discussion is the task of clarifying the issue, the goals for discussing it and the most appropriate process for that discussion. The more clearly an issue is framed, the easier it is for the group members to address it. Unfortunately, the person presenting an issue may not be able to clearly articulate his goals for the discussion. Further, he may be unaware of some of the broader implications the issue has for the group. Thus, the facilitator may need to talk to several people before the meeting in order to understand the dynamics at play and how to prepare for the group discussion.

Clarifying the issue may involve answering the following questions:
- Is the issue being raised a description of a problem that has been identified? If so, are there any solution ideas from the people identifying the problem?
- Is the issue being raised a proposal for a solution to a problem? If so, what is the problem the proposed solution seeks to solve?
- Is this an issue that needs a group decision? Is it an action item?
- Is it a need for communication? If so, what's the best way to meet this need?
- Who are the people most involved with this issue? Who are the stakeholders?
- Is this an issue for the whole group or some subgroup of involved parties?
- Should anyone outside the group be invited to the discussion?
- What is the history of dealing with this topic in the group?
- How does this history affect the context of raising the issue now?
- Is this issue a priority for the group at this time?
- How much time would the group be willing to devote to this topic?
- What is the timeline for the group to address this issue?

- Is there a deadline or a time-sensitive factor involved?
- Is the goal to begin dialogue or to reach a decision?
- What final decision rule would apply to a decision on this topic?
- Is there a general understanding of why this decision rule is appropriate?

These questions are important to consider prior to a group discussion. Sometimes the answers to these questions may indicate that a suggested topic is not actually appropriate for a group meeting. It may be a personal issue or an issue that only affects a subset of the group. There may be ways to handle the problem that are more direct than a group discussion. Meetings become decidedly more efficient when issues that do not need the group's attention are triaged without ever appearing on a meeting agenda.

If a facilitator suspects that an agenda item is not appropriate for the group, the situation should be handled carefully. The neutrality of a facilitator is jeopardized if she attempts to make a decision she is not empowered to make. Sometimes the situation can be handled by helping the person proposing the agenda item to choose a different way to address the problem. At other times, the facilitator may appeal to a person-in-charge for direction about whether to place the issue on a meeting agenda. If the authority to determine the agenda rests with the group, the facilitator may have to facilitate a group decision about the appropriateness of the agenda item, prior to officially discussing the issue.

Beth, a customer account representative, sent an e-mail to her manager, Margo, asking to have the topic "Fragrance policy" placed on the agenda for the next staff meeting. Margo dropped by Beth's cubicle to ask her some questions about the issue. Beth quickly placed a finger to her lips, indicating that she did not want to discuss the matter where the conversation might be overheard by Angela in the next cubicle. Margo obliged the request for discretion and asked Beth to come by her office later.

In the privacy of Margo's office, Beth expressed her desire for there to a be an office policy preventing anyone from wearing perfume to work. Margo asked Beth what problems she was observing that inspired this proposal. Beth explained that the only real problem was that she was repeatedly bothered by the scent of her neighbor Angela's perfume. She did not want to offend Angela by saying anything, so she hoped an office-wide policy might solve the problem.

With Margo's help, Beth began to think through the situation. She realized that Angela was likely to feel more offended by this indirect approach than by direct communication. Further, Beth realized that the rest of the office might get annoyed spending meeting time discussing an issue that only affected Beth and Angela. As an alternative, Margo offered Beth support in speaking directly to Angela. Beth then dropped her request for the issue to be put on the meeting agenda.

When a facilitator understands the suggested agenda item, he can help make sure it is presented to the group appropriately. Clearly defining the problem being addressed or the solution being proposed can help everyone understand what the discussion is about. Describing the goals for the discussion can also help group members know what outcome the group is being asked to work toward.

Knowing how important the item is to the group is also valuable. It can help the facilitator place the topic properly on the agenda. Crucial items may deserve a higher priority placement to make sure the group has time to cover them. Lower priority items may need to be tabled or delegated to an appropriate individual or committee to address.

Additionally, it is important to know if there are any group members whose participation in the discussion is essential. The meeting planning may need to accommodate the schedules of key participants.

Sometimes, in the course of researching an issue, the facilitator discovers that the issue is complicated by larger factors. For instance, confusion over the applicable final decision rule may indicate that a group has not clarified its decision-making authority. The organizational structure of the group may need to be addressed before the topic can be successfully resolved.

Controversial issues may also be complicated by interpersonal rifts within a group. Successfully discussing a topic might require first addressing an unresolved prior conflict. Perhaps some group members would benefit from mediation. Or perhaps the whole group would benefit from training in effective communication. Discovering these dynamics ahead of time can help a facilitator prepare for what types of intervention the group may need.

Finally, the facilitator must use all this information to determine what type of process the group should use to address each issue. Some agenda items may be routine. Time efficiency may be a high priority for dealing with them. A shortcut process may be appropriate. Other agenda items may be substantial or controversial. These items would probably benefit from the full CODM process. For particularly complex topics, multiple meetings may be appropriate, so that each stage of the process can be covered adequately without meeting for too long at one time.

Framing an Issue

The following points summarize the most important components of framing a topic for discussion:

- What are the goals of discussing this topic?
- Is a group discussion the best way to accomplish these goals?
- What group members need to be present?
- How much of a priority is this topic?
- How much time should be devoted to the discussion?
- What larger dynamics might impact the discussion?
- What process or shortcut should be employed to structure the discussion?
- What decision rule will apply to provide closure to the process?

Interview a Sample of Group Members

Interviewing a sample of group members is the best way a facilitator can discover how to frame an issue for group discussion. These interviews may be casual conversations. Or they may be more formal, depending on the size and culture of the group. Either way, these conversations strive to accomplish important goals. The facilitator is gathering the information she needs to understand how to frame the topic for the group.

The interviews are one-on-one conversations between the facilitator and a group member. While it might be more convenient to interview multiple participants at one time, this can be problematic. Anyone not included in such a meeting may feel left out of an important part of the process. Some government bodies have laws against informal subgroup meetings for this reason. Individual interviews provide a more discreet setting for participants to express themselves more openly. This helps the facilitator gain more insight into any underground group dynamics.

The first interview is usually with the person who has submitted an agenda item. In this discussion, the person proposing the topic is asked to self-reflect upon his reasons for bringing the issue to the group. Is the group being asked to make a decision? Is it being asked to rubber-stamp a decision that has already been made? Is it just being asked to hear concerns and offer understanding or appreciation? Is there a pressing problem to be solved?

Group members sometimes place items on an agenda because they need the group's attention in some way. There is nothing inherently wrong with this, as long as the request is clear and conscious. It does make sense to consider, however, whether attention to more personal needs is a welcome agenda for the particular group or not. Often, an individual may not be clear whether his goals are personal. Some thoughtful questions might help discern this.

Interview Questions
- "What have you noticed happening that makes you concerned about this issue?"
- "What concerns do you have about the situation you have observed?"
- "What goals do you hope to accomplish with the solution you are suggesting?"

- "What needs or concerns of yours would these goals address?"
- "Who else would be affected by the issue you want to discuss?"
- "What needs or concerns might each of them have?"
- "What kind of response are you looking for from the group?"
- "Are you wanting to be heard, or do you want the group to make a decision?"
- "To your knowledge, has the group dealt with this issue before?"
- "What makes it a good idea for the group to address this now?"
- "What feelings do you have about the situation you want to address?"
- "Would it be useful to you and/or the group to disclose your feelings and needs openly?"
- "So I am better prepared, is there anyone else I might talk to before the meeting to help me get other perspectives on the issue?"
- "Is there any informational research that would be useful for the group to have in discussing this?"
- "Do you have any concerns about how the group addresses this issue?"
- "Would you be willing to discuss with me how to open the discussion of this issue to the group?"

Dialogue between a facilitator and the group member who has suggested a topic can help ensure better presentation of the issue (whether the facilitator or the group member ultimately presents the agenda item). The goals for the group discussion can be clarified. And forethought can be given to the expected response of the group. The needs of the group may sometimes conflict with the needs of the presenter. For instance, some members of the group may not want to discuss the issue being presented. Giving some consideration to these dynamics can shed some light on how to best present the topic to the group.

Interviews with other group members are also important for several reasons. They can help a facilitator assess the level of shared interest or relevance of the topic. They can also reveal the true scope of the issue. Is it really a personal problem someone is having? Is it a simple group decision that needs to be made? Or is it a major organizational issue that would require a comprehensive approach to adequately address? These kinds of things are good for a facilitator to know before the discussion begins. Finally, these interviews can reveal what types of informational research would be helpful to prepare for the meeting.

Identify and Delegate Pre-Meeting Research

Pre-meeting research is the gathering of any information that might assist a group to understand an issue or come to a decision. For instance, consider a meeting of a nonprofit group sponsoring a teach-in on preventing gang violence. One of the agenda items might be "improving event attendance." For the group to discuss this topic intelligently, it would probably be valuable to have attendance figures for any of the group's recent events. This data could help the group understand the extent of any attendance problem.

The facilitator can help ensure that the group's needs are considered prior to the meeting. Part of this thinking includes asking what data, reports or background information would prepare participants sufficiently to make a group decision at the meeting. Good research preparation prevents groups from wasting time on hypothetical discussions that are later rendered moot once actual information is available.

To ensure follow-through, the facilitator can request that specific group members be responsible for collecting and providing the research the group needs. Delegating such tasks helps reduce the facilitator's workload. But it makes sense for other reasons as well. Certain group members may have better access to the information needed. Also, sharing the pre-meeting research tasks helps more people become aware of the issues to be discussed. As they do the research, they begin to think through the issue more fully. Delegating research tasks also gives more people a role in assisting the group and a chance to be appreciated for their contribution.

Introduce the Discussion

The final task in framing a topic is introducing the discussion to the group. This introduction describes how the discussion will proceed. The

Pre-meeting research is the gathering of any information that might assist a group to understand an issue or come to a decision.

facilitator's focus is on the process of the discussion, not the content. This should happen before a group leader, or the participant who proposed the topic, begins the ensuing discussion.

The key components of this introduction are intended to help orient the group members. They include:

- What the topic is
- What the goals for the discussion are
- What CODM steps the discussion will utilize
- The order of the steps
- The timeline for the discussion
- The way the decision will be finalized
- The reasons for using a consensus-oriented process

Covering these topics in a brief introduction can help all the group members understand the terms of the following discussion. If the group is familiar with the CODM process, of course, these points do not need to be outlined for each discussion.

Introducing a CODM Discussion

- "Our next topic is 'Developing Goals for the Coming Year.' The executive committee is asking the group to discuss this with the goal of defining a manageable set of goals for the group to prioritize next year. I suggest we use a consensus-oriented approach because this is such an important topic and everyone's participation is needed. The structure of the discussion I suggest follows the CODM model. This model helps everyone be able to participate and collaborate. And it also helps us keep progressing step by step toward a final decision.

   "The process starts with an open discussion, during which the group can generate as many ideas as possible. Then, we will get more systematic in identifying the major concerns we want our list of goals to address. After that, we will start to collaboratively explore how different goals might satisfy the concerns we have identified. This will help us we find out which goal statements generate the most agreement. Then, we will hone in on a proposal for a final list of the goals. Finally, we will see if this list we come up with receives the two-thirds majority that the group's bylaws say is needed for this type of decision. Is that clear? We have allotted four hours for this whole process, with a break in the middle. As we go along we can assess whether that time frame is workable.

"If anyone did not follow all that, you can see the steps on the process flowchart I put up on the wall over there. Is there anyone who has questions about the process we are about to follow?"

After the introduction, the facilitator can field any questions or concerns about the process. Following this, the facilitator may need to describe the structure of the first step, open discussion. Options for structuring this step are explained in the next chapter. Once the process is framed and the first step outlined, the group is free to proceed.

How Much Leadership?

As valuable as leadership is, too much leadership can be problematic. An overactive facilitator can rob the group of the opportunity to build a strong web of relationships with each other. Groups grow more cohesive when they succeed in working through differences together. A facilitator who mediates most potential group conflict through pre-meeting interviews may rob the group of the chance to work things out directly with each other. Such leaders may be valued and have good rapport with everyone in the group. The groups they facilitate, however, may never gel in a synergistic way, because the web of interpersonal relationships in the group is too dependent on the facilitator.

Each facilitator must therefore balance two goals. One goal is to help a group through a decision-making process as efficiently as possible. This is often the primary objective. Another goal, however, is to help group members learn how to do this themselves. Attending to this second goal requires teaching the group the skills you are using as a facilitator, so that a culture of skilled egalitarian leadership can grow. This second goal also involves helping the group members improve their relationships with one another. Both tasks take time. The more progress is made with the second goal, however, the more easily the first goal can be attained in the future.

Step 2:
Facilitating Open Discussion

Listen to anyone with an original idea, no matter how
absurd it may sound at first. If you put fences around people,
you get sheep. Give people the room they need.

WILLIAM McKNIGHT, 3M PRESIDENT

It seems to be one of the paradoxes
of creativity that in order to think originally,
we must familiarize ourselves with the ideas of others.

GEORGE KNELLER

Open discussion is the cauldron of group creativity. Once a facilitator has framed the issue and opened it for discussion, the group begins its work. In open discussion, the minds of the group members are stimulated by each other. Some ideas spring from what has already been said. Other ideas head off in completely new directions. The improvisational freedom of open discussion allows spontaneous genius and collaborative magic to naturally emerge. Under the right conditions, open discussion can be both exciting and very productive.

---

1. Inspire an open-minded, creative discussion.
2. Provide guidelines and structure for the discussion.
3. Manage the discussion.

4. Support full and varied participation.

5. Record the ideas generated on an Ideas Chart.

Step 2 of the CODM process provides an opportunity for open discussion. The job of the facilitator during this phase is to establish and safeguard the conditions that allow open discussion to flourish. The leader does not fix upon on the specific ideas being expressed. Rather, her attention is focused on the emotional atmosphere of the group. Open discussion is most creative and productive when group members feel that the ideas they express are appreciated, understood and safe from criticism. Generating this environment is the primary goal.

Inspire an Open-Minded, Creative Discussion

A facilitator can set the group in right direction by introducing some general principles of healthy, open discussion. Articulating the goals of safety, respect, participation and listening can be useful in conjuring an atmosphere where group members are more conscious of how their participation can support the whole group. If the group has a history of conflicted interactions, the facilitator can offer hope and a fresh vision to counter some of the negative dynamics that might otherwise emerge.

The facilitator serves here as an inspirational leader, a keeper of the faith so that with everyone's cooperation, a true spirit of collaboration is possible. Sometimes facilitators can use an inspirational quotation that invokes a heightened consciousness in the group. Consider the following quote from the Sufi poet, Rumi, as an example:

> Out beyond ideas of wrongdoing and rightdoing, there is a field.
> I'll meet you there.

Generating a safe atmosphere is a creative task. It is helpful for facilitators to share something that inspires them personally. Whatever principles, images, personal stories, famous examples or cross-cultural perspectives bring you to a higher state of consciousness can be used to inspire a group. What best reminds you to respect others and keep an open mind?

Provide Guidelines and Structure for the Discussion

Structuring a discussion is an important way to establish and maintain a safe group atmosphere. Open discussion can be either loosely facilitated or highly structured. The facilitator must determine the degree of structure that would best serve the group. Groups that are naturally respectful and supportive of each other may not need much intervention. When participants do not have good communication skills, or when group relationships are stressed, more structure may be useful. In groups with high levels of interpersonal tension, specific guidelines for behavior may be needed.

There are two rules of thumb about structure. The first rule is to provide as little intervention as is needed to keep the group atmosphere functioning well. The second rule is to make sure you do provide the intervention that is needed. The group needs you to lead when necessary—and to back off when the process is proceeding well without you. It can be difficult to gauge this fine balance, and you may err on one side or the other. By staying responsive to the reaction of the group, however, you can self-correct whenever necessary.

Open discussion is *open* because the content of what participants say is left undefined. Within whatever structure is used, group members can speak their ideas freely. They do not have to worry about whether their input follows logically or fits well with what has already been spoken. New topics and unrelated ideas can all go into the pot. Divergent thinking is encouraged. It serves to generate a broad range of ideas that enrich everyone's understanding of different perspectives.

The way in which people express themselves, however, is not open. In order for a healthy group atmosphere to prevail, the facilitator must intervene when participants interact in ways that erode the level of safety and respect in the group. The structure of the discussion sets a framework for how participants speak about whatever it is they want to say. If this framework is well constructed prior to a discussion, then the facilitator has a clear foundation on which to make any needed interventions.

Ground Rules

To establish structure, the facilitator can ask the group to agree to some ground rules at the outset of the discussion. If these guidelines are later breached, the facilitator can then intervene by reminding the group to stick to the agreements. When a facilitator knows that a topic will be contentious, a more comprehensive set of guidelines may be useful to prevent problematic behavior. When group members are already very connected to one another, it may be unnecessary to articulate specific ground rules. A facilitator who prepared for the meeting by interviewing a sample of participants will be better informed about what behavioral guidelines may be needed.

There are many possibilities for ground rules. The following list covers a wide range of options. Your intuition about what guidelines will be most relevant for your group can help you choose which of the following you present.

- Always speak from a place of respect for each other.
- Assume good intentions on the part of other group members.
- Respect differences of opinion and value the diversity of the group members.
- Practice open-minded listening.
- Speak honestly and openly.
- Speak only for yourself. Do not describe the thoughts or feelings of others.
- When describing the behavior of others, stick to objective, observable facts. Do not judge, interpret, exaggerate, generalize or caricature another's behavior.
- Do not label people or make generalizations based on stereotypes.
- Do not insult anyone personally or call anyone a derogatory name.
- Refrain from using non-verbal sounds to indicate disgust or contempt.
- Do not interrupt others.
- Do not use profanity.

- Think about the good of the whole group.
- When you feel angry or upset, breathe deeply to calm yourself.
- Ask questions when you sense conflict or misunderstanding.
- Raise your hand if you wish to speak. A volunteer can then make a list (*stack*) of those waiting to speak.
- Speak up if you have not been participating.
- Make room for others if you have spoken often.
- Allow a brief moment of silence to let the previous speaker's words sink in before the next person speaks.
- Designate a talking stick or other talisman that is placed in the middle of the group after each person speaks. When you wish to speak you first reach for the stick. No one speaks when they are not holding the stick.
- No one speaks twice until each person has spoken or had a chance to pass.
- Each speaker is limited to a specified amount of time, requiring them to distill their thoughts before speaking.
- No side conversations.

Unstructured Discussion

In addition to ground rules, several types of discussion structure are described below. These include brainstorming, go-arounds and facilitator-centered discussions. In smaller groups that function very comfortably, however, additional structure may not be necessary. If participants have the personal skills to support an engaging, divergent exploration of ideas without structure, then there is no reason to burden them with unnecessary rules. A facilitator can simply monitor the discussion, providing intervention only as needed.

One common intervention, even in unstructured discussions, is *stacking*. Stacking is a useful tool when several people wish to speak at the same time. The facilitator, or a designated stacker, keeps a list of the order in which participants request a chance to speak. Group members on the stack each get their turn in order. Stacking frees people to listen more carefully to others, rather than look for any available opportunity to interrupt.

If someone has a need for an immediate comment, they can request to interrupt the stack. The facilitator then decides whether to allow this. Generally, permission to interrupt the stack is granted, unless someone tends to abuse the option.

Another helpful practice in open discussion is recording participants' ideas on easel paper. This task is described later in this chapter. It is mentioned here because it is applicable to all of the following open discussion structures.

Brainstorming

Brainstorming is a very common discussion format to help a group generate a wide range of ideas and perspectives. In addition to any relevant ground rules, these guidelines can set the stage for a good brainstorming session:

- Each person gets a chance to speak her ideas, without interruption (except by the facilitator).
- Avoid criticizing, comparing or evaluating anyone else's idea.
- When you speak, it is to offer your idea, not comment on what has been said.
- Listen, and try to understand each other.
- Ask for clarification if you need it (without implying criticism).

Perhaps the most important aspect of brainstorming is the protection from criticism it provides people as they generate ideas.

Perhaps the most important aspect of brainstorming is the protection from criticism it provides people as they generate ideas. Critical analysis is a useful part of decision-making. But most people feel freer to explore ideas when they know their spontaneous thoughts will not be critiqued. Thus, in the service of generating a broad range of ideas, brainstorming guidelines ask participants to refrain from commenting on previously mentioned ideas.

An alternative to brainstorming is card storming. The difference is that in card storming ideas are written on cards instead of voiced to the group. The whole group takes some time for all the participants to write multiple ideas, each on their own card. The cards are later read to the whole group (usually without identifying who wrote the idea). This allows more safety for risky ideas to be offered. It can also help timid people contribute more

REFRAMING CRITICISM

Sometimes group members are unfamiliar with how to express their own ideas without criticizing other ideas. Even when asked not to, participants may critique previous comments. The facilitator can help maintain a non-critical atmosphere by reframing criticisms whenever they are inadvertently aired.

To reframe a criticism, the facilitator tries to identify what value a critical comment may have, independent from the idea it criticizes. There are several different types of value that any comment may offer. These include:

- Describing a problematic situation
- Identifying a relevant need or concern
- Proposing a possible strategy or solution

Even a critical comment, such as "That will never work!" can be reframed as an attempt to add value to the conversation in one of these three ways. The facilitator can steer the conversation in this direction by asking for this value to be offered without reference to previous ideas. Examples of this might be:

- Is there an aspect to this problem you want to make sure is addressed?
- Can you pinpoint the need you want any solution to address?
- Do you have an option you would like to add to the mix?

Answers to any of these questions will allow the value in the speaker's perspective to be articulated in a way that is independent from whatever has already been said.

Another useful concept in reframing criticism is the "yes and" mind frame. "Yes and" is a different way of responding to other people's ideas. It is in contrast to the "yes but" debates people commonly have. "Yes and" offers acceptance of the validity of what has been said before and then adds additional thinking. For instance, "That will never work!" could be reframed as, "Yes, that's a possibility, and here's another...." This mind frame promotes more collaboration than the "yes but" approach, which tends to negate the value of the ideas preceding it.

easily. The drawback is that the lack of interaction limits the ability of group members to stimulate each other's thinking.

Go-Arounds

A go-around is another way to structure open discussion. Again, the content of what people say is left open. In a go-around, however, the order in which people speak is structured. The structure of a go-around is very useful for ensuring that everyone gets an equal chance to speak. When a group has individuals who tend to dominate discussions, a go-around format can broaden the group's level of participation.

A go-around can be conducted in two ways. In the common *linear style*, the turn to speak passes around the table or circle from one person to the one next to him. A popular alternative to this is *popcorn style*. In popcorn style, each person takes their turn when they are ready (like kernels of popcorn randomly popping), but no one speaks twice until everyone has had a chance. An advantage of linear style is that the order is clear. A drawback is that participants may want to speak sooner or later than when their turn comes. In popcorn style, people choose their own time to speak, but there can be some awkwardness to the order. Sometimes no one is ready, and sometimes two or more people want to speak at the same time.

A *talking stick* or other type of talisman can be used to clearly identify whose turn it is to speak. This practice is common in many indigenous cultures. Whoever is holding the talking stick has the floor. When that person is done, she can pass the talking stick or place it where the next person can pick it up. Using a talking stick can heighten the quality of listening in a group discussion. It provides for a pause after each person speaks and the stick is passed. This pause allows the words spoken to resonate a moment before new ideas are offered.

Facilitator-Centered Discussions

Another option for structuring open discussion involves very active interaction between participants and the facilitator. Rather than speak to each other, each participant has a turn to engage in a conversation with the facilitator while the rest of the group listens. The facilitator uses reflective listening and asks clarifying questions to ensure that the speaker's point is clearly understood. This method is particularly useful when unstructured interactions between group members are tense or hostile. Some groups benefit from this style, however, even if the group is comfortable with one another.

The main benefit of facilitator-centered discussions is that a skilled facilitator can sometimes evoke more articulate contributions from group members than an unstructured discussion would allow. By focusing on one individual at a time, a facilitator can make sure that each person has a chance to have their point of view fully explored before the group moves on. The whole group, as it listens, can better understand each person when that person has the facilitator's help to fully express themselves.

REFLECTIVE LISTENING

Reflective listening (active listening) is a fundamental communication skill first described by psychologist Carl Rogers. In reflective listening, the listener responds to a speaker by either repeating or paraphrasing the speaker's message. Short sentences can be reflected verbatim. Longer expressions require a listener to capture the essential meaning in condensed wording. If the listener errs in accurately reflecting a speaker's intended message, the process is repeated until authentic understanding has been communicated.

Reflective listening seeks to accomplish two important goals. One, it is used to verify whether the person listening has accurately understood the person speaking. This is useful in a group, because often a speaker's message is misinterpreted by some of the other group members. A listener may be unaware, for instance, of certain assumptions a speaker may have. When participants discuss topics without actually understanding each other, the potential for confusion and conflict is increased. Reflective listening can clarify when a speaker's message is truly understood.

Secondly, reflective listening offers the speaker the experience of being understood. When the need to be understood is met, people usually feel a sense of satisfaction. This frees a speaker, who has succeeded in being understood, to turn her attention to understanding others. Thus, by carefully helping each participant feel well understood, the facilitator increases the capacity of the group members to really listen to each other.

One example of a facilitator-centered discussion is the Focused Conversation Method developed by the Institute of Cultural Affairs as part of its Technology of Participation (ToP™) program.[1] In a focused conversation, the facilitator guides participants through four types of questions:

- Objective "What did you actually see, hear or read?"
- Reflective "What was your gut level reaction?"
- Interpretive "What new insight did you get from this?"
- Decisional "What do you think we should do?"[2]

These four question topics have some common ground with the four components of Nonviolent Communication (NVC) developed by Marshal Rosenberg.[3] The teachings of NVC include many valuable communication skills helpful to any facilitator. To help people communicate clearly, NVC guides people in the following four steps:

- Observation "What actually happened?"
- Feeling "What emotion are you experiencing?"
- Need "What need of yours is affected by the situation?"
- Request "What actions might help you meet your needs?"

Either set of questions can be a useful template for a facilitator to help group members articulate their perspectives to the group. As each group member addresses these questions, everyone in the group develops a fuller understanding of the issue being discussed.

Another facilitator-centered discussion method is Dynamic Facilitation, developed by Jim Rough.[4] In this process, the facilitator converses one-on-one with group members throughout the meeting. By offering each participant a profound sense of understanding, observed by the group, Dynamic Facilitation seeks to generate a *felt-shift* in the group's whole approach to an issue. The process does not follow formal steps or employ any form of decision rule. It relies solely on open discussion. Participants can speak about whatever they choose, while the facilitator helps them deepen and clarify their message to the group. When the process is successful, the group emerges with a shared understanding of how to approach an issue. The facilitator then reflects her understanding that this shift has occurred.

OBJECTIVE OBSERVATION

Both Nonviolent Communication and the Focused Conversation Method begin with an important first step. To communicate well, one must be able to describe events in an objective way. Unfortunately, most people tend to exaggerate, generalize, caricature, use metaphors or judge the behavior of others, rather than simply describe the facts. The distortions usually are an attempt to justify whatever response we might have to the behavior we are reacting to. Unfortunately, when our description of another person's behavior is not objective, we are likely to evoke defensiveness rather than understanding.

When a facilitator notices that a group member is describing someone's behavior in ways that are judgmental or distorted, an intervention can be helpful. Simply ask the speaker to describe what they actually observed, as objectively as possible. Sometimes, however, this request must be repeated a few times before the speaker understands how their non-objective language may be unintentionally generating defensiveness in other group members.

This shift in the group's energy can make the remaining steps of a decision-making process go quite smoothly.

Facilitator-centered discussions rely heavily on a facilitator's communication skills. When these skills are strong, a facilitator-centered approach can generate a profoundly supportive group atmosphere. This is especially helpful when the group members are not able to provide deep listening for each other. The understanding that is engendered can improve relationships between group members. This method, however, does not directly address the ability of group members to interact with each other. Participants do not get a chance to practice the skills they see modeled by the facilitator. An opportunity to do so might help a group learn to function better when facilitation is not available.

Breakout Groups

When a group is too large to allow each person a chance to speak, breakout groups can allow everyone to participate. Dividing into separate groups gives each person more air time to articulate their ideas. In addition, small groups can be a safer atmosphere for people who might be intimidated to speak in a large group. The ideas generated in the small group can then be summarized and presented to the large group.

A good size for a small group is usually between four and ten people. Some facilitators believe six is optimal. Any method of dividing into small groups can be used. One handy method is to divide the total number of people by the number you want in each group. This quotient will tell you the number of groups to form. Then go around the group with each person counting off to that number. For instance, if you have 90 people and want 6 people in each group, you will have 90÷6, or 15 groups. To assign people to groups, have each person count off up to 15 repeatedly until each participant has a number. Then form small groups of the six people who all have the same number.

Fishbowl Discussions

Another option for large groups is the fishbowl discussion. In this format, a subset of the whole group conducts a discussion in the center of the room. Around them, the rest of the large group observes the discussion and takes notes. If the subset is chosen in a way that represents the large group well, then most of the ideas and concerns of the whole group will be expressed in the discussion. Afterwards, the larger group can be asked to add anything that has not already been mentioned. This format allows the whole group to hear the whole discussion, while reducing the amount of repetition. The selection of who will be inside the circle (in the fishbowl) must be made carefully. It can be done through a random selection process or one that uses specific selection criteria appropriate to the discussion. Sometimes it is useful to conduct a fishbowl with just two people in the middle. The whole group can then observe a poignant and condensed discussion between two people who represent distinctly opposing viewpoints.

More comprehensive formats for facilitating large group discussions are also available. One worthy of note is Open Space Technology, a large group facilitation design originated by Harrison Owen. While it is not specifically a decision-making process, it is a useful format for generating and sharing ideas among a large group of people.[5]

Manage the Discussion

Once the appropriate structure has been introduced, the group discussion can be opened. At this point, the facilitator's job is to manage the discussion to encourage a safe, positive atmosphere and full participation. When the group strays from the guidelines or when additional structure is needed, the facilitator should be ready to intervene to assist the group. Usually, the most effective intervention is simply to remind the group of the guidelines or structure and to request their cooperation. It is always best to clearly describe what you want group members to do, rather than criticize them for whatever they are doing.

- "Let's start with an open discussion that gets a variety of ideas out on the table."
- "Let's make sure that we give everyone a chance to speak and that we welcome all ideas at this stage, even if we don't agree with them."
- "Is the purpose of this step clear to everyone?"
- "I want to remind everyone about speaking your own idea, rather than commenting on someone else's idea. Does everyone understand the difference?"
- "Let's each pay attention to our non-verbal behavior, stuff like groans or eyeball rolling, so that we keep making the atmosphere safe for new ideas to be expressed."
- "Remember that we don't have to debate the merits of any of these ideas at this point. We just want to keep our brains churning creatively."
- "Is there anyone who has not said anything yet? We would love to hear whatever you are thinking."

Group facilitation becomes particularly challenging if one or more group members are uncooperative. Sometimes this is a sign that a decision the facilitator has made is out of step with the group. Perhaps the pace is too slow, or too fast, for some of the participants. If she senses resistance, the facilitator can query the group to discover if the process could be changed to better meet the needs of group members.

Sometimes, however, a group will have a member (or multiple members) who are particularly disruptive to the process. These individuals may have poor social skills or impaired sensitivity to others. They may have a tendency to dominate, filibuster, play the victim or otherwise manipulate a group. The facilitator should intervene with such people with a gradually increasing level of directness. Initial requests should be presented to the group as a whole, so as not to single out anyone in particular. If repeated attempts prove unsuccessful, the individual may need to be addressed directly. This can be done more discreetly during a break. Sometimes, however, it must be done in the midst of a discussion in order to immediately protect the group atmosphere. Unfortunately, the communication skills necessary to handle the most difficult cases are more than can be described here. A good understanding of Nonviolent Communication, however, would be very useful in these situations.

- "I notice, Bill, that you have added several ideas. In order to make sure others have room to speak, would you be willing to hold your ideas for longer and wait until I call on you before you speak again?"
- "Some of your comments, Andrea, have been about ideas other people have spoken. For this phase of the discussion, would you be willing to stick to generating new ideas rather than evaluating the ones already mentioned?"
- "Roger, can I ask use to use a softer tone, one that makes sure to carry the message that you respect the person you are speaking to? I want everyone to feel comfortable, and I imagine some people may be affected when the volume of a conversation goes up."

- "Juanita, I imagine you have been thinking about this subject as we have been discussing it. Would you let us know any of the thoughts you have been having?"
- "We have about 20 minutes left for this discussion and a lot of ground to cover. I wonder if everyone would be willing to distill the most important aspects of what they have to say before they speak. We can use time more efficiently if we offer the 'pearl' of our idea, rather than the whole story behind it."

Managing participation during open discussion often means raising the participants' consciousness of their effect on the group. Whether someone is quiet or dominating, their behavior affects the group. A caring facilitator can encourage self-reflection and behavioral change. By articulating principles of good communication and respectful interaction, a facilitator both shepherds the group atmosphere and gives participants an experience of healthy, functional interaction. The group can move toward a decision and learn to communicate more effectively at the same time.

Support Full and Varied Participation

A facilitator can enhance the safety and creativity of the group by supporting group members to fully participate. Supportive responses help participants feel understood and valued. These good feelings motivate group members to participate and generate more ideas. Modeling support is also a way for the facilitator to demonstrate how group members could respond to each other. When support begins to flow freely in a group, the members generally experience the meetings as a very enjoyable and bonding experience.

Validating that there is a legitimate need behind an idea is a good way to stay positive and supportive of group members even when one of their ideas is a true clunker. Most of the unworkable ideas expressed in an open discussion do not need to be critiqued. They will not find a champion to carry them into the next phases of decision-making anyway. The star ideas will shine and the stones will sink on their own. So, to keep the discussion flowing, the facilitator makes brief supportive statements and then moves on.

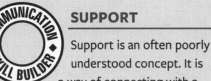

SUPPORT

Support is an often poorly understood concept. It is a way of connecting with a person who is expressing himself. It has two main components. The first is reflective listening, described earlier in this chapter. A listener uses reflective listening to clarify her understanding of the speaker's message and to help the speaker feel understood.

The second component of support is validation. Validation is the message that the speaker or the speaker's ideas have value. Receiving this message can be very comforting. It helps a speaker feel appreciated, in addition to feeling understood. When a group member expresses an idea, the facilitator can reflect back what she understands to be the crux of the idea, and then validate some way in which the idea makes sense or has value. Validation, however, must be authentic. When the value of an idea is not authentically understood, the listener can ask questions that lead toward this goal.

As discussed previously, almost all ideas expressed by group members are an attempt to add value to the discussion. The types of value offered include describing a problem, identifying a need and proposing

an option. If a facilitator can identify any of these three motivations, they can validate the speaker's contribution. For instance, a facilitator might respond to the comment "That whole department is a total mess" by saying, "You are seeing that there are some complicated problems, and that a really comprehensive solution might be necessary. Is that right?"

It is possible to find value even in comments that are not phrased positively. Speakers sometimes criticize others, rather than identify and ask for what they need. Often people are unaware of their needs. A facilitator can help a participant identify the unmet need or unsatisfied concern behind their remark. Bringing this need forward adds value to the group discussion. Thus, a facilitator can support a group member by understanding the underlying need at issue and validating the importance of addressing that need. For example, a group member might say, "Nobody ever tells me what's going on until they want something from me yesterday!" This person could be supported by identifying the need underlying her complaint. A facilitator might respond with "You are identifying a need for more planning and/or more communication. Is that right?"

A product development team held a meeting to establish the general specifi-
cations for a new software application. After multiple necessary components
had been suggested, some of the group members began to feel overwhelmed
at the amount of work that developing the new product would require. One
member then suggested, quite seriously, that the group simply steal already
established code from a rival product. Others in the group were aghast at the
speaker's blatant disregard for ethics. In order to keep the brainstorming on
track, the facilitator quickly offered some support for the idea, saying, "Steal-
ing code? Okay. That would certainly meet our need to reduce our workload.
Any other ideas?"

Offering support for ideas can be overdone. Not everyone needs to hear
validation of his idea. Further, no one wants to hear inauthentic support.
Thus, a facilitator should monitor when offering support would be useful
and when it might actually get in the way of the group.

The facilitator should also be looking for other ways to encourage full
participation. A safe, supportive atmosphere is not always enough to get
everyone to contribute. Sometimes the facilitator will need to coax reluc-
tant group members to participate. This can be done by direct request, such
as "We haven't heard from Don or Yvonne yet. Would either of you two be
willing to offer your perspective?" Or participants might be prodded less
directly with a general request, such as "Every idea that anyone in the group
has is like a piece to a big puzzle. You might not know how it fits in when
you first look at it, but it's good to get all the pieces out on the table. Is there
any piece, no matter how small, that hasn't been spoken yet?"

Record Ideas

Recording the ideas that the group generates is an ongoing task during
open discussion. The facilitator can do this herself, but the job may dis-
tract her from attending to the group members. Often, the person recording ideas has his back to the group as he charts the ideas he hears. Thus it is

preferable to have a designated chart writer serve as the recorder. The chart writer should be able to write legibly and quickly. It is also best when the recorder is skilled at capturing the essence of a wordy idea in a short phrase.

The ideas expressed by the group can be recorded on large easel paper, labeled "Ideas Chart." As each page is filled, it can be posted on a wall visible to the whole group. Having a visible list of ideas is helpful for several reasons. It makes the whole range of ideas expressed by the group immediately accessible. Our brains can only hold so many ideas at one time. Posting idea lists is like increasing our RAM (a computer's random access memory). It helps us increase the information immediately available to us. The Ideas Chart generated in open discussion will continue to be helpful throughout the CODM process, as well. The group can refer back to it when it begins developing proposal options and when it synthesizes the details of a final proposal.

Figure 6.1. A Simple Template for an Ideas Chart

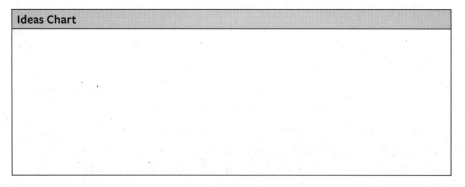

There are several helpful chart-making practices worth noting. Charting is a skill and emerging profession of its own. Some people bring an impressive artistry to the task. Fun graphics can be a valuable contribution to the group atmosphere. Even modest recorders, however, should keep the following points in mind:

- Whenever possible use the participants' own words. This communicates respect and reduces the potential for misinterpretation or biased recording.

- Take note when there is repetition of an idea. Ask whether the repetition is an indication of the importance of the idea. Keep in mind that ideas that sound similar sometimes have subtle variations. Encourage participants to articulate any uniqueness to their contribution.
- Ask permission when grouping or combining ideas. Grouping can be useful, but it can also focus the group on analyzing existing ideas instead of generating new ideas. If it interrupts the flow, grouping or combining ideas can be done later.
- Do not search for *the right idea*. Just record them all, knowing there is some value in each one.
- Do not attribute authorship to any idea. Collaboration is enhanced when the group owns all the ideas. Attributing authorship only stokes competitive and territorial feelings.
- Establish a *parking lot* on your chart or on a separate paper. This allows you to record off-topic suggestions without interrupting the flow of more closely related ideas.

Summary

In sum, during open discussion the facilitator offers inspiration to the group to interact with each other in ways that keep the atmosphere safe for creative and divergent thinking. She then structures the discussion with a variety of possible ground rules and discussion formats, depending on the needs of the group. The facilitator maintains a positive environment by intervening to reinforce the discussion guidelines. She also offers support to group members and encourages full and varied participation. The Ideas Chart generated during this discussion is the tangible product of this step. It will be referred to throughout the rest of the decision-making process.

Step 3:
Identifying
Underlying Concerns

If you want to build a boat, do not instruct the men to saw wood,
stitch the sails, prepare the tools and organize the work, but
make them long for setting sail and travel to distant lands.

Antoine de Saint-Exupéry

In Step 3 of the CODM process, the group identifies the fundamental concerns people have about the issue being discussed. In doing so, the group develops its mission for the discussion. The underlying concerns, identified in this step, establish the criteria that will guide the rest of the process. If the group can develop proposals that effectively address all the underlying concerns, a successful decision will emerge.

1. Ask the group to identify all the stakeholders affected by the issue.
2. List all underlying concerns of each stakeholder on an Underlying Concerns Chart.
3. Gather all the identified concerns to form the basis for collaborative proposal development.

Identify Stakeholders

Anyone likely to be affected by a group's decision is a stakeholder. And each stakeholder may have particular concerns about an issue before the group. Sometimes there are only a few stakeholders. A women's book club, for instance, may appear not to have any stakeholders other than the group members themselves. A closer look, however, might identify the families of the women as stakeholders, if they are affected by the club's meeting schedule.

At the other end of the spectrum, a large organization may have many types of stakeholders: board, staff, volunteers, funders, the population served and the larger community. And some of these categories may have distinct subsets of stakeholders. To keep track of them all, the facilitator or chart writer can list stakeholders as the group identifies them.

Often, there are stakeholders who are not members of the decision-making group. The concerns of these parties are likely, however, to be important considerations in the group's decisions. Thus, these stakeholders' concerns are identified in this step along with all the concerns that group members themselves may have. Hopefully, group members are able to identify external stakeholder concerns accurately. If not, some research into this area is likely to be useful. If the need for research is identified prior to the meeting, preparations can include gathering information from external stakeholders. If the needed information is not available during the meeting, the group may have to postpone a decision or make a tentative decision based on further research.

Sometimes a large issue will have multiple stakeholder groups. There may not be a single organization that contains a majority of the stakeholders. Developing government policies, for instance, may require the involvement of several different interest groups. Convening meetings that gather input from disparate and sometimes conflicting organizations requires careful planning and advanced facilitation techniques designed for multi-stakeholder decisions. Both Open Space Technology[1] and CODM can be useful tools for such situations.

To save time at a meeting, a preparation committee can identify stakeholders and their primary concerns. The results can be presented to the group for review. The group can then add any missing stakeholders or concerns. While this shortcut can save time, it does have a potential drawback. The group may passively accept the committee work without fully participating in a comprehensive search to identify stakeholder concerns. Potentially, an important concern may be overlooked.

Identify Underlying Concerns

Once the stakeholders are named, the group can begin identifying the concerns that each of them may have. On large easel paper, the facilitator can construct an *Underlying Concerns Chart*. On the chart, list each set of stakeholders at the top of a column. Then, as the meeting progresses, list all the underlying concerns identified for each stakeholder.

FIGURE 7.1. Underlying Concerns Chart

Stakeholders						
Concerns						

Usually, the group will not follow a linear order as it identifies concerns. A suggested concern of one stakeholder will be followed by a suggestion of a separate concern of another stakeholder. Eventually, however, the list under each stakeholder grows. Naturally, the most involved stakeholders will end up with a longer list of concerns. Some concerns may be shared by multiple stakeholders. This can also be creatively noted on the chart.

Here are a few definitions of terms used in this chapter:

Stakeholder: Any person or group of people affected by a decision the group may make

Position: A specific plan or strategy to solve a problem that is advocated by someone

Underlying concern: A need or problem people are seeking to meet or solve

Need: A universal human desire for satisfaction

Strategy: A plan for how to meet a need (similar to "position")

Positions vs. Underlying Concerns

There is an important distinction between a *position* and an *underlying concern*.[2] A position is a specific plan that someone may advocate. It is a solution proposal or strategy. An underlying concern, in contrast, describes a problem that needs a solution. An underlying concern addresses questions such as "What problem do we want to solve?" or "What need do we want to satisfy?" A position statement answers the questions "How do we solve

FIGURE 7.2. The Difference Between Positions and Underlying Concerns

Position	Underlying Concern
We should hire an accountant.	We need to keep track of our group's finances in an understandable way.
Let's have a moratorium on adding new members.	I'm concerned about the size of our group and the impact of new members on the group's sense of intimacy.
We have got to meet regularly.	I'm worried about people feeling disconnected and decisions being made haphazardly.
I propose that we focus on the upcoming election for the next two months.	I'm concerned about how the election might affect our work. And I'd like to be clear about our current priorities.
Let's increase the commission we give to the salespeople.	We need to boost sales somehow.

this problem?" or "How do we meet this need?" Examples of the difference appear in Figure 7.2.

Differentiating positions from concerns is a common practice in mediation. Parties usually come to the table with their positions in mind. For instance, the union representative may want a 5% raise for the workers, and the management may want to switch to a cheaper health care plan. Both of these are positions. To identify the underlying concerns, the facilitator asks: "What do you hope your plan will accomplish?" or "What needs will your proposal help satisfy?" Possible answers from the union representative might include "We need to earn enough to pay our rent" or "We need to be treated with dignity." The management might reply: "We need to reduce expenses so that we can stay in business" or "We want to spread our cost reductions out so that no one is treated unfairly."

Once the underlying concern beneath a position is identified, alternatives to the position become imaginable. If a 5% raise is not possible, how else can rent be paid and dignity be upheld? If reducing health care coverage is not agreeable, how else can the company reduce expenses in a way that treats people fairly? Options begin to open when underlying concerns are identified. This is usually much more productive than arguing over a finite number of positions.

Sometimes the facilitator must ask participants to self-reflect to find underlying concerns. When a group member is strongly invested in a particular position, she may not easily see her underlying concerns. For instance, a school board member may insist upon replacing a school principal. When asked what problem this would solve, her answer might be "Well, then we'd be rid of him." Deeper questioning is needed to fully identify the relevant concern. The dialogue might go as follows:

Facilitator: What would be better about getting rid of him?

Board member: Well, then we wouldn't have to deal with him anymore.

Facilitator: And what is hard about dealing with him?

Board member: He's a pain in the neck.

Facilitator: How does he make your job harder?

Board member: Well, he never prepares anything before he meets with us.

Facilitator: So one concern is the need for preparation to make meetings go better. Is that right?

Board member: Yes. But there's more.

Facilitator: Okay, what else?

Board member: Well, he also fires good teachers without having anyone to replace them.

Facilitator: So you have a concern that staff decisions be made more carefully?

Board member: Yes.

Identifying underlying concerns creates room for options. If the board member above cannot convince the board to fire the principal, then her position loses and the problems she has identified may continue. On the other hand, if the group works together to address the specific concerns, then the situation can improve, whether or not the principal stays. As a group identifies the underlying concerns of any issue, the options for dealing with those concerns can be approached with greater creativity and collaboration.

Underlying Concerns and Human Needs

Underlying concerns are usually based upon unmet needs. Articulating feelings and personal needs, however, is more vulnerable than voicing concerns. Often it is difficult for people to identify feelings and needs. There are many societal messages that discourage this level of vulnerability. As group members raise concerns, they are probably identifying important human needs, even if they do not describe them as such.

A background understanding of human needs can help a facilitator discern when a group member has identified a fundamental need (rather than voicing a position or strategy).[3] It can guide a facilitator in deciding when to question participants more deeply. The main criterion for determining whether someone has identified a need is the question of whether the experience is universal. Do most humans have this need? You have definitely identified a need if you are confident that almost anyone would feel better with that need met.

For example, an alcoholic may feel like he needs a stiff drink at the end of each day. His wife, however, may not share that experience. The lack of universality suggests that a stiff drink is really a strategy, not a need. The need he is trying to meet might be relaxation. Everyone enjoys relaxation. That need is universal. If the alcoholic can identify all the needs he meets by drinking, he may begin to identify other strategies to meet those needs.

Whenever someone talks about needing a specific person to do a specific action, the principle of universality tells us that the need referred to is really a strategy. I might think I "need" my wife to tell me she loves me. But not everyone needs my wife to say this to them. Nearly everyone, however, does need to feel loved. So my need is to feel loved. And getting my wife to tell me she loves me is one strategy for meeting that need.

The table below lists many universal human needs, under several general categories. It is not intended as a comprehensive list. But studying it can help you improve your understanding of human needs and how they

FIGURE 7.3. Universal Human Needs

Physical Needs	Food—Hunger; Water—Thirst; Clean Air; Rest—Sleep; Right temperature; Freedom from pain/injury; Relaxation—Tension release; Exercise—Movement; Release of sexual charge; Human touch
Mastery	Accomplishment; Effectiveness; Creativity; Growth; Order; Efficiency; Organization; Competence
Connection	Attention; Positive regard; Listening ; Empathy; Communication—Self-disclosure; Authenticity—Honesty; Affection; Love—Caring; Acceptance; Security; To be seen and heard; Trust; Inclusion; Cooperation; Respect; Humor; Fun
Autonomy	Freedom; Personal choice; Inclusion in decisions; Equality; Solitude; Boundaries; Space
Meaning	Purpose; Spirituality; Universal/Spiritual relatedness; Direction; Contribution; Growth; Self-expression; Self-esteem
Safety	Freedom from threat of injury; Freedom from the threat of other needs going unmet
Other Needs	Novelty; Beauty; Stability

differ from the positions or strategies someone may use to try to meet these needs.

Facilitators can use whichever term they prefer, *needs* or *underlying concerns*. The choice may depend upon what level of vulnerability the group is comfortable expressing. It is good to respect a comfortable degree of emotional openness for the group. There may be legitimate reasons, such as significant power dynamics, behind why group members may prefer less vulnerable language.

Regardless of the term used, the important task in this step is to identify the fundamental goals that each stakeholder may have. Listing them helps the group see underneath any specific positions or strategies that may have been suggested. Once all aspects of the problem are more clearly understood, new, creative solutions can be better formulated.

Gather All the Concerns

During this step the group will have created a list of all the underlying concerns of each of the stakeholders. Considering each stakeholder's concerns separately, however, would foster a process where everyone must advocate for their own concerns. Such discussions can become competitive. Solutions that meet some needs are pitted against solutions that meet other needs. The goals of collaboration are not met by this type of discussion.

The facilitator, therefore, prepares for the next step by suggesting that all the concerns be metaphorically gathered into the same basket. All needs are considered together, owned by the whole group. The focus of the group proposal building is then directed toward satisfying all of the concerns raised, as much as possible.

- "Okay. Now that we have all the concerns we can think of listed, I want to ask you something. Do you think we could all work as one team to try to think of solutions that would satisfy as many of these concerns as possible?"
- "Now usually a discussion might involve so-and-so arguing for these concerns and so-and-so defending the importance of those needs. I'd like us

to try something different. Instead, I want us all to build solutions together that are designed to meet all the needs identified here, no matter whose needs they are. Are you up for that?"

- "So does everyone agree that the best solution we can come up with will be the one that most satisfies as many of these concerns as possible? And to the extent that we are successful at that, we will have a solution that everyone is on board with. Does that make sense?"

- "Imagine for a moment that we all committed to trying to come up with solutions that satisfy all of these concerns. This means that you don't have to worry about individually advocating for the concerns you care most about, because you know everyone in the group wants to satisfy those concerns too. Imagine yourself thinking about concerns that you do not personally have, and making sure they are addressed in the final proposal. Do you think we could all take on that perspective? Would you be willing to try?"

Gathering all the concerns together presents a compelling challenge to the group. The facilitator can voice this challenge in a way that inspires the group to work together. The request is that group members change their perspective from one of "I need to make sure the concerns I have get addressed" to one of "Together we are going to try to figure out how to satisfy all of these concerns to the greatest extent possible." This difference is a big paradigm shift for some people. It asks them to stop thinking solely of their individual concerns and to start thinking about how all the stakeholders can be best satisfied. When the facilitator is successful in inspiring this type of thinking, the group's potential for synergy makes a quantum leap. Let's sum up this step by looking at an example.

A meeting was held by North County Organic Farmers (NCOF), a nonprofit group organized to support local organic farming. The meeting agenda included deciding what sort of community outreach event the group might host to raise the community's awareness and support of organic farming.

The open discussion from the previous step generated the following list of ideas:

Figure 7.4. NCOF Event Ideas Chart

Ideas Chart
Picnic
Battle of local bands competition
Speakers
Mayor speech
Video on organic farming
Hoedown
Potluck
Farm customer sign-ups
Pie eating contest
Slide show of local farms

In this step the group was first asked to identify stakeholders. They came up with the following list:

- NCOF staff
- Local organic famers
- People already supporting organic farming
- The larger community

Then the needs and underlying concerns of each stakeholder were identified, resulting in the following chart.

Figure 7.5. Underlying Concerns Chart

Stakeholders	NCOF Staff	Farmers	Supporters	Public	Other
Concerns	Not too much work Build membership Generate donations Gain visibility Enough time to plan Teach the public	Sign up new customers Sell some produce Not compete with each other Support NCOF	Get together and have fun Not be bored Not work	Have fun Be attracted by the event Learn Not be captive audience Easy to get to event	City has permit requirements Park neighbors may object to noise

Once these underlying concerns were identified, the group was asked to consider putting all of these concerns in the same basket. They were challenged to begin thinking of how all the stakeholders' needs could be met as much as possible. Some of the NCOF staff began to realize that meeting the needs of the public was essential to the whole project. Some of the farmers, who had elaborate visions for the event, began to realize that the plan had to be realistic for the small staff at NCOF. And the farmers also realized that keeping the event non-competitive was a goal that affected how farmers might attract customers or sell produce at the event.

Summary

In this step the group identifies stakeholders and their underlying concerns. This prepares a group for building creative solutions. It establishes the criteria those solutions must meet to be successful. In the Chapter 8, we'll look at how to build those solutions collaboratively. Once that step is explained, we'll follow the example above to the next stage.

Step 4:
Collaborative Proposal Development

Once you know what you want to accomplish, it's time to start developing your best options. In the CODM process, the group tackles this job together, acting as a single team throughout the step. Gone are the rancor-filled, competitive debates over whose idea is better. Instead, the facilitator keeps the group focused on one option at a time, working together to develop each option to its highest potential.

---

1. Describe the collaborative process of taking turns to build multiple proposals.
2. Help the group select root ideas on which to develop proposals.
3. Use a Proposal Development Chart to help the group develop each option to its full potential.

People who have not experienced working collaboratively may not believe it is possible. Before a meeting, I sometimes hear resistance to the CODM process, based on the idea that competition sharpens people's thinking or that some amount of fighting over a topic is inevitable. Personally, I enjoy competition. I love to play soccer and tennis. And I appreciate it when my opponent's skill challenges me to perform better. But competitive debate is another story. I do not enjoy being interrupted, having my point distorted so it can be discarded, enduring a filibuster or being subjected to the many other tactics that can be used to win a debate.

Much of what goes on in a rigorous debate actually harms relationships. Winners may get the decision they wanted, but group members suffer from increased animosity toward each other, due to the power tactics used in the process. Losers, who were outfoxed, may resent the winners either for their superior debate skill or for their manipulative tricks. Further, the voices of some people in the group drop out when the discussion turns adversarial. More sensitive people do not feel safe to engage when their ideas may be directly criticized. As these people drop out of the discussion, so does their wisdom, creativity and unique perspective.

CODM avoids the pitfalls of competitive debate by staying collaborative all the way through the process. In this step, CODM takes a page from the history of collaboration on the American frontier. Settlers on the prairie needed barns on their farms. But no single family could raise the walls and roof of a barn without help. If they each competed to see which family could build the biggest barn, there would be no barns at all. Instead, they employed the most basic lesson of every kindergarten: they took turns. Neighbors gathered to build a barn for one family, then did the same for the rest of the neighborhood.

Here are some definitions of terms used in this chapter:

Idea: Any suggestion that emerged in the open discussion or afterward

Root ideas: The suggestions chosen by the group to provide the foundation for building proposals

Option: A root idea that is being developed into a proposal

Proposal: One possible comprehensive plan to satisfy as many of the group's concerns as possible

Collaborative process: A group taking turns to jointly develop one option at a time

Describe the Collaborative Process

It is important for a facilitator to clearly describe this step before beginning. Otherwise, habitual patterns of argumentation may emerge. In a nutshell, this step involves selecting a few basic ideas (*root ideas*) and growing them into possible solutions. Each root idea gets a turn, wherein the whole group builds on the idea until it addresses as many identified underlying concerns as possible.

The facilitator helps by keeping the group focused, fully participatory and inspired to collaborate. Some participants may resist participating in developing options that they already know they don't support. It is important for the facilitator to encourage people to shift from this perspective to one of greater open-mindedness. While there may be some who remain stubborn, most group members enjoy exhibiting their intelligence and creativity in the service of a group project. Motivation can increase when a participant realizes that his assistance in improving a rival idea will be returned when the group helps to fully develop his favorite option.

- "So now we are going to develop some of the ideas we have into possible solutions. We are not making any decisions yet. And I hope everyone is staying open-minded, even if you might already have some preferences. We will pick a few ideas and give each one a turn. During that turn, I would like the whole group to try to think of how to build that idea into the best solution it can become. That means you help improve the idea, even if it isn't your favorite idea. Are you willing to try this?"

- "Instead of debating these ideas and having people defend or criticize each one, I'd like to try a collaborative way of working together. Before we decide anything, I want to make sure we have the best possible options to choose from. So I want everyone to work together to develop several different ideas. We will try to figure out how each one can satisfy all of the underlying concerns we came up with. Then, after we have done that with several ideas, we will move to deciding which option we like best. How does that sound?"

- "You might already know you like one idea better than the others. But all these ideas have room to grow. And the group needs everyone's intelligence and participation developing each option we consider. That means I am asking you each to help improve ideas you might consider to be rivals to your own idea. That's collaboration. If we can take turns doing that, this group can really start being creative."

Select Root Ideas to Develop

To begin this step, the facilitator guides the group in selecting which ideas, developed in open discussion, are promising enough to form the basis of a possible proposal. The group can choose how it will select these root ideas and how many it will consider. Time is usually an important factor. If time is limited, the group will probably need to select only two or three of the most popular ideas. If the decision is very important, however, then the group may be willing to spend more time and consider more root ideas.

Ideas that are not selected as root ideas are not discarded. They remain available to be incorporated into any proposal under construction. For instance, if the group of organic farmers in the example from the Chapter 7 did not choose "pie eating contest" as a root idea, the concept could still become part of a proposal built upon the idea of hosting a harvest festival. Most of the ideas from the open discussion session will retain this potential even if they are not selected as root ideas.

Root ideas are generally chosen because their selection suggests a significant direction for a proposal. They lay a unique foundation or have a distinct theme. Usually, root ideas are not easily compatible with each other. If they are, then they can be developed as one proposal, not two. For instance, "harvest festival" would likely be a separate root idea from "May Day festival." Either option might incorporate some of the same activities, but it would not make sense to have a harvest festival in May (unless you are in the Southern Hemisphere).

The selection process for root ideas can vary. It can be formal or informal. Two factors help the group make this choice in a relaxed fashion. One, most ideas are still eligible to be part of proposal development. And two, additional root ideas can be chosen later if the group is not satisfied with the options it has developed. The facilitator can remind the group that no decision is final at this point. The group can always consider additional root ideas if need be. The three most common methods of selecting root ideas are a *quick poll*, an *advocate system* and *multi-vote approach*.

Quick Poll

A quick poll is simply a hands-up vote on any idea nominated by a group member to be a root idea. Group members can vote for as many ideas as they like (though they should be reminded that the more ideas considered, the longer the discussion will take). Depending on the time available, the group can then decide, informally, how many of the most popular ideas to address. This decision is informal because it too can be reversed later if there is a significant change of heart about how much time to give the decision.

Advocate System

The advocate system selects root ideas based on which ideas have at least one person in the group to champion the cause. This method often produces a higher number of options to be considered. To counter this, group members can be limited to sponsoring only one idea each, or sponsorship could require two or more advocates.

In either system, the facilitator can be very helpful to the group by advising on the selection of root ideas. When ideas are easily compatible, the facilitator can suggest that they not both be selected as separate root ideas. And when an idea is nominated for a vote, the facilitator can ask the group whether it represents a basic direction for a proposal or whether it is a detail that could be incorporated in proposals built from other root ideas. If the status quo enjoys some support in the group, the facilitator should suggest that it be chosen as one of the root ideas to consider.

Multi-Vote Approach

In large groups there are other options for selecting root ideas. One popular one is the multi-vote approach. This method allows participants the ability to vote for several options using round colored stickers (sticky dots). The root idea options to be selected can be posted on sheets of paper taped to the walls around the room. Each participant then receives a fixed number of sticky dots to place on the root ideas they favor most. They can do this however they wish. People usually enjoy milling around, discussing the options with each other and placing their dots. One helpful rule of thumb: divide the number of options by four to determine how many dots each person receives.

To save the full group's time, a proposal development committee can be tasked with developing proposal options. After the group generates ideas in open discussion, the topic is tabled. Then, a committee, informed by the group discussion, develops options to present to the group. When they are presented, the full group can revise these options or develop additional ones. This shortcut requires that a group meet twice, with committee work taking place in between meetings. The potential drawback to this shortcut is that the full group may accept the committee options without truly engaging the creativity or diversity of everyone.

Develop the Options

The process of building an option into a proposal can be easily structured by using a *Proposal Development Chart*. This chart is constructed by listing all the underlying concerns the group previously generated down the left-hand edge of a large piece of easel paper. To the right of each concern, list any idea the group has for how that concern could be satisfied. There are two examples of Proposal Development Charts in the case example below.

The guiding question for this step is "How can we satisfy all of the concerns as much as possible?" Everyone in the group is tasked with generating suggestions toward this goal. There can be multiple suggestions about how to address each stakeholder concern. As in a brainstorm, it is not necessary to dispute suggestions. For example, the need to raise money at an event could be met by an admission fee or by a raffle. The choice between these options does not need to be settled at this stage. Making a detailed choice at this time would be an inefficient use of time, given that the overall proposal being built may not even be chosen. The specifics of the final proposal will be worked out in a later step. The purpose of this step is simply to discover what potential each proposal has to satisfy the group's goals for the decision.

As an example, let's look at how the organic farmers and their organization NCOF (North Country Organic Farmers) developed the root ideas "harvest festival" and "hoedown." Each root idea was built into a proposal by filling in a chart (see the following page).

These two options were built on different root ideas, harvest festival or hoedown. As the group developed each chart, they more clearly understood how each of the options might address the group's goals. Many of the original ideas from open discussion were applicable to either option and were included on both charts. Other ideas were workable for only one of the options.

While there were some participants excited about dancing at a hoedown, the charts led most people in the group to conclude that a harvest festival would allow more of the group's goals to be addressed. This option was then chosen as a direction for a final proposal. As the details were finalized in a later step, the harvest festival became the group's official choice. The idea of a hoedown, however, was kept open as a possible event for the upcoming winter.

Facilitate Option Development

The facilitator can offer a group valuable assistance during this barn-building process. Drawing the charts, each with the same list of stakeholder concerns, helps keep the discussion focused on the task of satisfying those concerns. The charts make it very clear what concerns still need suggestions.

Figure 8.1. Harvest Festival Proposal Development Chart

Concern	Possible Ideas		
Not too much work to produce the event	Get farmers to help	Keep it simple	Use newsletter to recruit volunteers
Doable timeline	No problem		
Build NCOF membership	E-mail sign-up	Have a free drawing for prizes	Bring a friend – Get free fruit
NCOF visibility	Banner	Publicity: Radio, newspapers, posters	
Generate donations	Short speech		
Educational	Booths with info		
Farm customer sign-ups	Each farm has a booth	Have a single e-mail sign-up sheet that all farms will have access to after the event.	Have NCOF e-mail out a list of all the farms after the event.
Selling produce	Each farm has a booth		
Not competition between farms	One big booth with all the farms sharing equal square footage		Don't sell produce
Fun for supporters	Pie eating contest	Hay ride	Music
Interesting for supporters	Composting workshop		
No work for supporters	Keep it simple	Hire an event coordinator	
Enticing to public	Pitch to families	Free food	Hot air balloon
Easy to get to	Downtown park	Sunnyside Farm	Lakeview Farm
Permit obtainable if needed	Easy	Research hot air balloon idea	
Neighbors' concerns	Daytime event should not be a problem		

FIGURE 8.2. Hoedown (evening) Proposal Development Chart

Concern	Possible Ideas		
Not too much work to produce the event	Get farmers to help	Just need a dance band and an info booth	
Doable timeline	No problem		
Build NCOF membership	E-mail sign-up	Have a free drawing for prizes at intermission	
NCOF visibility	Banner	Publicity: Radio, newspapers, posters	
Generate donations	Short speech during break		
Educational	Booth with info in lobby	Brief talk during inter-mission	Video on a TV in the lobby
Farm customer sign-ups	Tables in the lobby	Have a single e-mail sign-up sheet that all farms will have access to after the event.	Have NCOF e-mail out a list of all the farms after the event.
Selling produce	Not so easy at night		
Not competition between farms	One big booth with all the farms sharing equal square footage		Don't sell produce
Fun for supporters	Dancing, music	Old-timey costumes	
Interesting for supporters	Dancing, music		
No work for supporters	Keep it simple		
Enticing to public	Get a good band	Free hot food	Fun for singles too
Easy to get to	Downtown park	Odd Fellows Hall (may be too small)	Civic Hall (expensive?)
Permit obtainable if needed	Need to check on this		
Neighbors' concerns	Park noise may be problem at night. End early?		Talk to neighbors to get support?

The process can be both orderly and thorough, but it remains creative and collaborative. The facilitator continues to address the group atmosphere to ensure that it feels safe, open-minded and supportive of all suggestions.

After each chart is filled in as best it can be, the facilitator moves the group on to the next root idea. A new chart helps the group develop each idea into its own proposal.

Since many ideas are applicable to several different proposals, the process may accelerate as it progresses. New proposals are developed more quickly because they can import some ideas from previous proposals. Likewise, new ideas that emerge for later proposals may be applicable to earlier proposals. These new ideas can be added to the previous charts.

As the charts are filled out, the group members gain the information they need to make a thoughtful choice. Displaying all the concerns and all the suggestions as to how to meet those concerns is a very effective way to help the group evaluate the potential of each proposal to accomplish the group's goals. In this step, the group develops its best options as well as it can. And it has also prepared itself for the next step, choosing the direction for a final proposal.

Step 5:
Choosing a Direction

It's in your moments of decision that your destiny is shaped.

Anthony Robbins

Making a choice can take courage. Many people have difficulty with decision-making. Sometimes the hesitation to choose has a rational basis. More time, more ideas or more research may be needed. But sometimes the hesitation is due to fear. Fortunately, the previous steps of the CODM process provide a group with a solid basis on which to decide how to move forward. The Proposal Development Charts the group has produced provide a detailed account of how the solutions under consideration might work. Now, in order to progress, the group must choose which direction has the best chance for success.

---

1. Check for readiness to choose a direction.
2. Analyze the proposal options.
3. Use preference gradient voting to choose which option to develop further.

In this step, the group chooses a single proposal to develop further. Unless this decision is later reversed, the group will focus exclusively on the chosen proposal for the rest of the discussion. Only after this proposal is finalized in a later step, however, does the group make a formal decision as to whether the proposal is adopted.

Check for Readiness to Choose a Direction

The choice of a single option is a significant step. So it makes sense to ask the group if it is ready to proceed. If there is hesitation, the facilitator can spell out the group's available options:

- Devote more time to developing the existing proposal options.
- Select an additional root idea and develop it into another proposal option.
- Table the issue, so people have more time to think about it or gather more information.
- Delegate the choice of options to a committee.
- Analyze and then choose which proposal to concentrate on developing further.

Describing the finite set of process options listed above can clarify each person's preference. Additionally, the facilitator can describe the next steps of the process. This helps participants understand that the decision in this step is not final. The proposal voted on can still be amended. And everyone retains the option of voting against the proposal after it is further developed.

- "We've done some great work developing several proposal options. Now it's time to select one of them and see if we can improve it even more. After that, you will have a chance to vote on whether you favor the final proposal or not. We could conceivably pick a proposal to finalize and then later vote it down. If that happens, we can always choose another option and see if we have better luck getting broad support. If we pick a good one now, however, then we will only have to do the following steps once. Are you all ready to analyze these options and then vote on which one we should select?"

- "I see there is some hesitation to move toward selecting one of these proposals to work on further. Is that because people sense that we don't have enough options or enough information? Can anyone put words to the hesitation so we can understand it?"
- "So it sounds like most people are ready to start narrowing the options. But a few of you are hesitant. Perhaps we could move on to the analysis of these options and then check again to see if everyone is ready to take a vote on which one has the most promise."

The CODM process helps groups move toward decisions by gradually narrowing the focus. First, a few root ideas are selected from the broad list of open discussion suggestions. Then, after developing these root ideas into proposal options, one is chosen for further development. Each of these steps is reversible if need be. This reassurance can encourage the group to move forward. As each step is taken, however, the group members gradually adjust to the fact that a decision is evolving.

If the group is not ready to move on, the issue can be delegated to a proposal development committee. The group's collaborative effort will likely serve as a valuable guide to a committee tasked with further researching the proposal options and recommending one for further development. Such a committee may serve the group by giving the proposal options more thoughtful consideration than the group may have time for. Delegating further analysis to a committee is often more effective than trying to push forward with an unprepared group.

Analyze the Proposal Options

Prior to voting on the proposal options, group members will need a chance to freely advocate for their preferences. Up to now, the discussion has been structured to remain collaborative. Criticism has been discouraged, and the group has been tasked with working together to make each proposal option the best it can be. Thoughtful critical analysis of the options, however, has a valuable place in decision-making. And this is the time.

A go-around is a useful structure for this part of the discussion. Giving each group member a chance to speak, one at a time, has multiple benefits. It encourages full participation. It prevents people from interrupting each other. It helps make sure everyone is heard. And finally, it prevents any single group member from dominating the debate.

The two common formats for conducting a go-around are described in the following paragraph from Chapter 6:

> A go-around can be conducted in two ways. In the common *linear style* the turn to speak passes around the table or circle from one person to the one next to him. A popular alternative to this is *popcorn style*. In popcorn style, each person takes their turn when they are ready (like kernels of popcorn randomly popping), but no one speaks twice until everyone has had a chance. An advantage of linear style is that the order is clear. A drawback is that participants may want to speak sooner or later than when their turn comes. In popcorn style, people choose their own time to speak, but there can be some awkwardness to the order. Sometimes no one is ready, and sometimes two or more people want to speak at the same time.

If the group is large and time is short, the analysis of options can be done by a subset of the group. A single representative from each set of stakeholders, for instance, might have a turn. Or, speaking may be limited to group members with particularly relevant expertise. In large public meetings the speakers may be chosen by lottery or by a first come–first served sign-up list. If there are distinct factions in the discussion, the available speaking time can be allocated in a way that provides balanced representation of the different camps. Separate sign-up sheets for each faction can assist this. Often, whether the group is large or small, an agreed-upon time limit for each speaker is useful.

The facilitator can focus the go-around by posing the central question of the analysis: "Which option has the best potential to satisfy all the concerns as much as possible?" It is very useful to write this question on a board where everyone can see it. If anyone's comments stray unproductively, the facilitator can shepherd them to return to this question. Usually, the analysis will hinge on two matters of personal opinion:

- Guesses about how well specific concerns will be satisfied by different proposals
- Preferences about which concerns are higher priorities

These opinions will play a large part in each person's view of which proposal is most favorable. There is likely to be some variety of opinion expressed. Fortunately, the group does not have to agree on each point. They will be selecting a proposal in the upcoming vote, but their reasons for supporting their choice can vary. Therefore, not every idea needs to be debated. Hearing each person analyze the options from their own perspective, however, is a good way to digest the main issues. The group's best thinking is brought forth for all to consider.

- "Before we vote let's give everyone a chance to tell the group how they would analyze these options. Here's the question I want you to answer: "Which option has the best potential to satisfy all the concerns as much as possible?" We can go around the group so everyone gets a chance to speak without interruption. If you have a lot to say, you might want to make notes for yourself so you make sure you cover all the points you want to. Please try to be concise. After everyone has spoken once, I'll check to see if there is more to say."

After the go-around, the facilitator can assess whether a second go-around would be useful. Limited time, however, may be a factor to consider. If there is no second round, it might be courteous to offer the option for a few volunteers to speak a second time. Sometimes it is hard to say everything you need to say when you only have one chance. Participants who spoke at the beginning of the go-around may be particularly in need of a chance to speak again.

Finally, before proceeding to a vote, the facilitator should check to make sure everyone understands the options to be voted on. Some people may be confused by the idea of voting on a *direction* for a proposal, rather than voting on a final proposal. The facilitator can make this distinction clear, noting that the proposal can still be refined before a final vote.

Preference Gradient Voting

After a thoughtful analysis, the group will probably be ready to vote. CODM uses a preference gradient voting technique in this step. *Preference gradient voting*[1] provides more information than "yes/no" votes or "choose your favorite" votes. These latter options may work for making a choice, but they may not accurately measure the strength of the group's choice. Because CODM's goal is to generate as much agreement as possible, it uses a voting system that more clearly measures the degree of support each proposal has.

In preference gradient voting, participants are asked to gauge their support for each option separately. On a scale of 0 to 5, participants can indicate the strength of their opposition or support for the option being voted upon. The vote can be taken by open ballot (show of 0–5 fingers) or by secret ballot (writing the number on paper). Open ballot is quicker and usually preferable, unless there is some reason that true opinions would be more accurately obtained through secret ballot. Figure 9.1 shows what level of support is indicated by each number of fingers.

FIGURE 9.1. Numbers in Preference Gradient Voting

Number	Degree of Support
0	I strongly oppose this option.
1	I oppose this option.
2	I lightly oppose this option.
3	I lightly support this option.
4	I support this option.
5	I strongly support this option.

The show of fingers can be a satisfying expression of one's opinion. Those strongly opposed can strike a fisted hand into the air. Those in strong support can spread their hand and five fingers widely. And the people who are more ambivalent have a way to show their more nuanced stance.

A *spectrogram* is another way to conduct a preference gradient vote. Instead of voting with fingers, the group members vote with their bodies. The facilitator designates one end of the room as the zone that represents "I strongly support this option." The opposite end of the room is designated as the zone that represents "I strongly oppose this option." Then participants are asked to get up and stand somewhere along the imaginary line between these two zones. They align themselves along a continuum. People who feel ambivalent should stand somewhere in the middle. A spectrogram is a quick way to get a very visual assessment of group support/opposition to a proposal. It can also be fun for participants to get out of their seats and vote with their whole body.

Each option is voted on separately. And each person is free to give their choice of support regardless of how much support they give to other options. For instance, a person who enjoys the status quo might vote 0 or 1 on all the options, hoping that none will gain enough support to carry forward. Another person might strongly support one option, but also show moderate support for another.

The results of this vote show how strongly the group believes in the potential of each of the options. The data can be useful in several ways. First, the average score for each option can be calculated and compared to the average score of each of the other options. Such comparison might indicate a clear winner. There are, however, other factors to consider too. Preference gradient voting allows the following points to enter into the analysis:

- Which option received the highest (or highest average) score?
- Is the highest score high enough to indicate strong support?

- Is there a close second?
- Of the highest scores, do any have strong opposition (votes of 0 or 1)?
- Is there strong support or opposition from any key players?

Each of these factors may affect which option the group should proceed with. Is it more important to have broad support and minimal opposition? Or is it more important that certain key players are enthusiastic about the option? Sometimes the outcome of a preference gradient vote is clear. At other times, the outcome provides valuable information, but no clear decision.

When the results of the preference gradient vote are not clear, the group will need the facilitator's help to move forward. The first step is to conduct a brief discussion to analyze the results of the vote. "What did the preference gradient vote tell us about which option to proceed with?" is the key question. After the cogent points have been sufficiently aired, the facilitator can assess whether there is general agreement on how to proceed. If there is not, a more decisive process must be applied.

To resolve any dispute or ambiguity over how to proceed, the facilitator can invoke the group's final decision rule. If the group operates by majority or supermajority, then an either/or vote is taken on the top two options. If the group has a person-in-charge who makes the ultimate decision, then that person is called upon to decide. It is important to clarify that this is a process decision. It determines which proposal the group will continue to develop. It is not a final decision to adopt the proposal as the will of the group.

- "It looks like we have two options that have strong support. One scores a little higher, but it has some people with strong opposition and some with strong support. The other one has broader support and less opposition, but less strong overall support. So this preference gradient vote gave us good information, but not a clear winner. We will have to decide between these two options. But first let's hear from anyone who wants to speak to the question of what this vote tells us about how to proceed."

- "Well, we have an option that outscores the others. But its average score is not really that high. It got a 2.4, which means the group as a whole is leaning ever so slightly away from this option, even though it's our best one. Does this mean that we really don't have a good option yet? Should we just stay with the status quo? Or do you want to develop this option further and see if we can make it into something that gets more support? Let's talk about that a bit, and then Melissa, as the business owner, you can decide whether you want the group to develop this option further."

If the group makes decisions by unanimity, then the facilitator must query any participants who object. Based on the objections raised, the facilitator then formulates a suggestion for how the group might circle back in the process to a point where the objections can be addressed. Are more ideas needed? Do some ideas need more explanation? Is there a vital concern that is still unsatisfied? Are there new concerns that are only now emerging? Hopefully this inquiry will help the whole group develop an option they can agree to carry forward.

Delegating the issue to a proposal selection committee can also be a useful way forward. If the group's analysis of the results of the preference gradient vote is not conclusive and if there is hesitancy to make a formal decision about how to proceed, the group may prefer to allow a committee to deliberate the issue. Once the committee chooses a direction for the final proposal, their choice can be brought back to the group. Delegating this important choice, however, does place significant decision-making power in the hands of the committee. As in all shortcuts, some degree of full participation is forfeited.

Manny, a software development team manager, found himself very stressed by multiple requests from the employees he supervised. Everyone wanted to be able to telecommute at least part-time. After trying to handle requests on an individual basis, Manny found himself surrounded by conflict on the issue. People were frustrated when others were not present for key meetings. People were frustrated when they had to come to the office on days they wanted to work from home. And people were frustrated that permissions were granted in ways that seemed arbitrary and unfair. The common wisdom was that if you pushed Manny hard enough, you could get what you wanted. But sometimes you had to push pretty hard.

Manny decided to try using the CODM process to come up with a policy on telecommuting that would address the problem. The group started by identifying three stakeholders: the engineers, the manager and the company. They then identified a number of underlying concerns. After this, they engaged in some open discussion and generated some key root ideas. (They inverted the order of the steps, but still made good progress.) The root ideas were then built into the following Proposal Development Charts. They all knew the company's main concern was their productivity. They considered that concern a given and did not include it in the charts.

FIGURE 9.2. Idea #1: Have a Standard Telecommuting Schedule for Everyone

Concerns	Possible Ideas	
Relief for Manny from the pressure of requests	Fixed schedule for everybody	
Fairness	Same schedule for everybody	
Having people at meetings	Same schedule for everybody	
Getting to work from home as much as possible	Two regular days per week of telecommuting	Tuesday and Thursday?
Flexibility to work some weekends and later take long weekends	Tuesday and Friday?	Don't have meetings on Fridays

FIGURE 9.3. Idea #2: Fixed Number of Telecommuting Days Per Person

Concerns	Possible Ideas	
Relief for Manny from the pressure of requests	Use your days as you like, but no extras when you are done	
Fairness	Everybody gets the same number	Some could get more if they have families
Having people at meetings	Schedule meeting in advance and require attendance	
Getting to work from home as much as possible	Maybe eight days a month?	Use your days to your best advantage
Flexibility to work some weekends and later take long weekends	Use your days to your best advantage	Don't have meetings on Fridays

FIGURE 9.4. Idea #3: Keep the Current System

Concerns	Possible Ideas	
Relief for Manny from the pressure of requests	Manny gets better at setting limits	
Fairness	Manny gets better at making the requests he grants more equitable	People could realize that everybody has different (not equal) needs
Having people at meetings	Schedule meeting in advance and grant no permissions	Send an e-mail every afternoon about any meeting for the next day
Getting to work from home as much as possible	Let Manny know what you need	Manny should give permission unless there is a reason not to
Flexibility to work some weekends and later take long weekends	Let Manny know what you need	Manny should give permission unless there is a reason not to

The preference gradient voting on these options resulted in the following scores:

FIGURE 9.5. Preference Gradient Vote

	Darlene	Lou	Jean	Dave	Carl	Hamid	Manny	Average
Idea #1	3	1	2	4	1	4	5	2.8
Idea #2	3	1	5	2	3	4	2	2.8
Idea #3	3	5	2	4	5	2	0	3

Manny asked the group to analyze these scores. Most agreed that while Idea #3 had squeaked by with the high score, it had a serious problem. Its success depended primarily upon efforts by Manny, who hated the idea. Hamid asked why Lou and Carl were so opposed to Idea #1. Lou responded that he was really just wanting to make sure he could have some flexibility in taking Fridays off so that his family could go on ski trips. He didn't mind working Saturdays on other weekends in return. Carl agreed that flexibility was the issue for him too.

Darlene then asked why there couldn't be a fixed schedule with a very limited number of exceptions that could be negotiated. Dave thought that was a great idea, calling it a combination of Ideas #1 and 3. Manny saw the heads nodding around the table and concurred that if there was a fixed number of exceptions that people could request, then he could support the idea.

The group then set to work on developing Idea #1 in a way that allowed for some negotiated flexibility. This effort constituted the essence of CODM's Step 5. Rather than experiencing a distinct step, however, the group slid right into synthesizing a final proposal without a need for formal acknowledgment that a process decision (selecting an option to finalize) had been made.

The ability of a group to choose a direction for a final proposal is enhanced by skillful facilitation of the CODM steps. The steps gradually narrow the discussion and help participants evolve their decision in stages. The facilitator consistently safeguards the group atmosphere, keeping it respectful and collaborative. By supporting group members, helping identify underlying needs and concerns, and inspiring the group to work together, the facilitator clears the path to a decision.

The more time spent in earlier steps—generating ideas and carefully understanding each other—the greater the level of agreement the group is likely to reach. When people feel that their ideas are heard and understood, they are less fixed in their positions. They become more open and amenable to supporting the prevailing direction of the group. Making a decision together becomes easier.

Step 6:
Synthesizing a Final Proposal

An invasion of armies can be resisted,
but not an idea whose time has come.

Victor Hugo

There is no good idea that cannot be made better, once the commitment to doing so is clear. In the sixth step of the CODM process, the group's intelligence converges upon a single proposal, shaping it into final form. In some ways this step is a review of all the previous steps. It includes remembering any unsatisfied concerns, brainstorming new ideas to address them and choosing which of those ideas generates the most agreement. But in this step, the stakes are higher. The proposal being finalized may soon become a decision. So any missing piece must be discovered. And any group member who is not satisfied must speak.

---

1. Review any unsatisfied concerns.
2. Identify details that might improve the proposal.
3. Select which details to include in the proposal.
4. Compose final wording for the proposal and a process for deciding any unresolved details.

The goal of the CODM process is to generate decisions that garner as much agreement as possible. Reaching this standard is the goal of this step. There is a danger, in group decision-making, that the concerns of some of the participants will be ignored once a required minimum threshold of support is reached. A majority-rule group, for instance, may vote and pass a proposal once the winners have 51% support, rather than going for greater agreement. This complacency, however, results in decisions that may ignore important issues. Effective implementation of these decisions may also be hampered when significant portions of the group do not feel their concerns were given sufficient attention. CODM goes beyond the goal of finding a proposal that will pass and strives for a decision-making process that includes everyone.

Sometimes the general direction of the final proposal is more important to the full group than the details. In this case, the group may elect to delegate decisions about the details to a final proposal committee. This committee might consist of the people primarily involved in implementing the decision. Delegating work to a committee can save the full group from the time-consuming process of making many decisions on minor details. After choosing a committee, the group can move on to the closure step and complete the full group portion of the process. Alternatively, the group can ask the committee to bring a final proposal back to the full group in a later meeting. At that time, the group can review and amend the proposal before moving to closure on the decision.

Review Any Unsatisfied Concerns

In previous steps, the group has discussed different options and chosen one to develop into a final proposal. Now the group has a final chance to address any underlying concerns that remain unsatisfied. The first question in this step is, "What concerns do we need to address to make this proposal even better?" The facilitator can address this question to the whole group. The people least supportive of the option, however, are likely to be the most aware of the ways the proposal falls short of widespread agreement.

The facilitator can draw out any resistance to the proposal by focusing questioning on whomever can best articulate the unsatisfied concerns. Is there a need that has not been addressed? Are there any concerns that were not identified before? Is the proposal likely to actually satisfy the concerns it is intended to address? Do the solutions involved cause other problems?

- "Let's hear from anyone who has doubts about this proposal. What are the concerns you still have? Is there anything that you don't think will pan out as planned? Are there any stakeholders that may not get what they need? Now is the time to voice these things, so we can see if we can work together to make this proposal as favorable as it can be."

As the group answers, the facilitator can offer support to encourage deeper reflection. As in the open discussion phase, this support can both reward participation as well as clarify the group's understanding. The facilitator can reflect back whatever concern is raised to verify if the speaker's point is accurately understood. And then the facilitator can validate whatever contribution the comment offers the group. These skills are described earlier in Chapter 6's Communication Skill Builder on support.

Identify Details That Might Improve the Proposal

The final proposal is synthesized by choosing the details that make it a more comprehensive solution. This task was begun in the barn-building step, but some group members may have held back then. They may have preferred another option and (out of laziness or competitiveness) resisted the appeal to cooperate in developing each option. When it begins to look like there is no turning back, however, even self-interest dictates that those who opposed the option should now work towards improving it. Sometimes new ideas are freshly generated. Sometimes ideas that were previously rejected are reconsidered.

The facilitator can help cultivate a spirit of reconciliation. She may encourage the participants who favor the proposal under construction to show support for addressing the remaining concerns of those opposed. This can shift the emotional dynamics. When people feel cared about and respected, they may soften their opposition. Likewise, the participants who are resistant to a developing proposal can be asked to express their understanding of the benefits the proposal might offer. The facilitator can help by reminding everyone that their long-term relationships with each other are probably more important to the success of the group than any particular decision. When the group's consciousness shifts in this direction, new creativity can emerge.

The Croxton city council held a community forum to debate a proposed bike path across some undeveloped greenbelt land the city owned. The crowd attending was largely split between those who favored the bike path as a way to ease traffic and improve bicyclist safety and those who wanted the land to remain completely undeveloped.

After a few opening speeches from advocates of each side, the facilitator asked speakers to more directly address the concerns of the other side. Cyclists were asked to address the problem of the very limited alternatives for experiencing a completely natural setting in the local area. Anti–bike path advocates were asked how traffic and safety concerns could be addressed without the path.

Despite the request, speakers from both sides tended to minimize the concerns of the opposition as they tried to persuade the council. One speaker chided the value of "meditating in the woods" versus saving lives in traffic accidents. In return, the opposition cited a lack of respect for nature as the most pressing concern in the modern world.

Rather than let the meeting polarize further, the facilitator asked the council to consider what had been said and indicate informally whether it was leaning toward or away from the bike path proposal. The council reluctantly agreed to conduct a straw poll using preference gradient voting. The result was strongly in support of the bike path.

The facilitator then presented a new challenge to the assembled public. "Rather than continue to debate whether or not to have a bike path, could we now focus the discussion on how to address the important concerns of preserving natural spaces as much as possible in a plan that includes a bike path?"

Most of the remaining speakers spoke to this question in an increasingly collaborative tone. There were a few exceptions: individuals who could not adjust their approach, even when it was clear their preference was unlikely (or already secure). Many speakers from both sides, however, generated ideas for open space protection in response to the facilitator's challenge.

Toward the end of the evening, one speaker who had voiced opposition to the bike path offered his support to the council members that favored the plan. He requested, however, that they promise to more seriously consider purchasing additional greenbelt land on the other side of the town. The mayor agreed to put the idea on the agenda for the next meeting.

The experience demonstrates how making a decision in CODM-like stages can help group members converge their efforts. By identifying the direction the council was headed, most of the open space advocates were able to shift toward building their concerns into the proposal at hand rather than risk fighting it, only to lose and alienate potential future allies. Likewise, the bike path advocates found they could assist rather than oppose many of the goals of the opposition. Doing so helped make their plan even more popular in the end.

Select Which Details to Include in the Proposal

As suggestions for how to improve the proposal emerge, the group must decide which ideas to adopt. This process may include making numerous small decisions about details. The central question in each of these decisions is, "Does this detail improve the proposal?" The most expedient decision method is for the facilitator to use his intuition to sort ideas based on the likelihood of the group approving them. This obviates the need to hold a vote on every detail. Ideas expected to be unpopular can be respectfully acknowledged but not pursued. Ideas that appear popular can be confirmed with a quick question, "Does that sound good to people?" The facilitator should remind the group that anyone is free to object. And he should be alert to the possibility of participants passively agreeing to something they do not actually support. If there are objections, the idea can be subjected to a more formal vote. Preference gradient voting will once again provide more information about the degree of support an idea enjoys. Simple pro/con votes, however, can be conducted more quickly.

If any details prove to be controversial, the decision-making process about them may need to be more formal. Sometimes, this means invoking the group's final decision rule (majority, supermajority, unanimity or person-in-charge). Often, however, a useful approach is to delegate difficult decisions on details to a subcommittee. This allows the group to maintain its momentum toward a collaborative decision on the main body of the proposal.

Compose Final Wording for the Proposal and a Process for Deciding Unresolved Details

Group decisions will usually benefit from very clear official wording. Otherwise, people may remember the decision in different ways. Formally wording the final proposal can prevent confusion down the road. It can be tedious, however, to deliberate final wording with the whole group. Once the concepts are clear, it is often useful for the group to take a break and allow a spontaneously convened committee (or individual) to develop the final wording. Alternatively, if the atmosphere is informal, the proposal can be decided upon in general terms, and specific wording can be finalized and distributed to group members after the meeting.

- "So our final proposal reads: 'The church will begin offering two services every Sunday starting in April, on Easter Sunday. The start times of these services will be worked out by the two ministers and the service coordinator. The latter service will experiment with including some ideas from the Young Adult Committee, as long as they promise not to change too much too fast. Pastor Thomas will oversee the process. And we will discuss how it

is going at our next congregational meeting in June.' Is this clear to everyone? Did we forget anything? ...Okay, let's make a formal decision on this."

The final wording should include any provisions for deciding details that
remain unresolved. If any issues have been delegated to a committee, it
should be clear what those issues are, who will serve on the committee and
how they will complete their work. If any provisions of the decision hinge
upon information that was not known at the meeting, the relevant con-
tingencies should be spelled out. Sometimes, if key assumptions prove in-
correct, this may mean discussing the issue again. Documenting all these
details in concise language can be challenging, but the effort is rewarded in
greater clarity going forward.

Improvising the Steps to a Final Proposal

By this point in the process, the group has accomplished a lot. Whether or
not the final proposal is adopted, it represents the best effort of the group to
work together. The CODM steps provide an outline for getting to this point.
Often, however, a group finds its way to this point through various shortcuts or modifications of the CODM process. Sometimes, certain steps are
completely skipped in order to proceed quickly to a decision. Each group
must decide how thorough they need to be in discussing a particular issue.

The facilitator helps the group make this decision by consistently assess-
ing the mood of the group and the importance of the discussion. Sometimes
the group mood may be impatient, but the discussion is still very important.
In this case, the group may just need to take a break. At other times, the
impatience of the group is a sign that they are ready to skip forward and
complete the process more quickly. While there is some risk involved in
skipping steps, a group may decide to accept this risk in the name of ex-
pediency.

Figure 10.1 outlines how the CODM steps progress with or without modifications, shortcuts or skipped steps.

FIGURE 10.1. CODM Steps and Alternatives

	CODM Steps	Shortcuts	Skipping the Step
STEP 1	Frame the Issue: The facilitator can prepare for the discussion prior to the meeting	A proposal presentation committee can present the group an analysis of underlying concerns and fully developed proposal options for the group to consider.	If there has been no preparation, the group can start discussing an item, figuring out the goals and relevance of the issue as part of the discussion.
STEP 2	Open Discussion	A routine decision shortcut may proceed from Open Discussion to Choosing a Direction and then Synthesizing a Final Proposal.	If creative thinking is less important, the group could skip Open Discussion and proceed directly to identifying stakeholders and their concerns.
STEP 3	Identify Underlying Concerns	A preparation committee may present an analysis of stakeholders and their underlying concerns.	If underlying concerns are readily apparent, the group could skip this step and start considering proposal options.
STEP 4	Develop Proposal Options	A proposal development committee can be delegated to generate options and report back to the group in a later meeting.	If a particular idea generates widespread support, the group may skip directly to synthesizing this idea as a final proposal without considering other options.
STEP 5	Choose a Direction		If there is no dissent, a group may seamlessly move from developing an option to synthesizing it as a final proposal without ever voting to do so.
STEP 6	Synthesize a Final Proposal	A final proposal committee may be delegated to work out the details of the final proposal.	If the details are not important to the whole group, they may be left undefined. The people implementing the decision may then work out these details as the need arises.
STEP 7	Closure		If the group prefers to leave a decision open-ended, the final proposal may not ever be officially adopted or rejected. A more informal outcome may result from the discussion.

11

Step 7:
Closure

Reconciliation is more beautiful
than victory.

VIOLETA BARRIOS DE CHAMORRO

Closure is the last stage of group decision-making. It includes officially finalizing the decision. It can also include attending to the feelings any group members may have about either the outcome or the way the decision was reached. Closing discussions well is an important way to maintain good group cohesion and positive relationships. A satisfying closure to a decision also sets the stage for good cooperation as the group implements its decision.

---

1. Apply the group's final decision rule.
2. Optional: Provide empathy for any unsatisfied participants.
3. Optional: Ratify acceptance of the group decision.
4. Optional: Request cooperation in implementing the decision.

The overall health of the group is more important than any decision the group makes. Even wise decisions may fail without a well-functioning group to implement them. Unfortunately, the struggle to make a decision can sometimes stress the relationships between group members. No matter how well the collaborative process has minimized conflict, there can be hard feelings and disappointments. In this final step, the CODM process attends not only to finalizing the decision. It also outlines optional processes for healing any emotional upset about either the decision or the process of making it.

Apply the Group's Final Decision Rule

Closure begins with a clear acknowledgment that the group has made a decision. The facilitator can help provide this clarity by applying the group's decision rule and announcing the result. Hopefully the group has already established a standard decision rule (majority, supermajority, unanimity or person-in-charge) or a special decision rule for this issue. If not, there may be some confusion at this stage. The group may have to choose a decision rule before it can finalize a decision.

Closure begins with a clear acknowledgment that the group has made a decision. The facilitator can help provide this clarity.

If there is broad support for the final proposal, the decision-making process may be less formal. Assuming that the requisite parties are present, the facilitator may simply read the final wording of the proposal and ask the group two questions:

- Is there general agreement to adopt this proposal as a decision of the group?
- Is there anyone opposed?

If there is unanimous approval or the required degree of majority, then the facilitator can simply declare the decision made. This should be recorded in the minutes, if someone is taking them, with the final wording of the proposal.

If the decision-making authority rests in a person-in-charge or a governing subgroup, then finalizing the decision will depend on their consent. Their presence is highly recommended for the full CODM process. If they are present, their consent can be assessed along with the rest of the group. If the decision makers are not present, however, the group's proposal can be presented to them after the meeting for final approval.

Optionally, a final preference gradient vote can also be taken. The results of a new poll can be compared to the results of the poll taken in Step 5, prior to synthesizing the final proposal. This comparison can show how effective the previous step was in strengthening the proposal and generating broader agreement. This effort is really only warranted, however, if there is sufficient curiosity about the matter.

If the final proposal is not approved, the group has two choices. It can consider the matter closed and allow the status quo to remain in effect. Or, it can circle back to an earlier stage in the CODM process to generate an alternative final proposal. Does the existing proposal need only a few changes in detail? Could an alternative proposal be built on a different root idea? Or does the group need wholly new ideas to begin with? The facilitator must assess the group's commitment to continue. Unless there is sufficient support for renewed efforts, the decision is over.

Provide Empathy for Any Unsatisfied Participants

Once a decision has been made, there are several optional activities that can help a group experience a more profound experience of closure. Providing empathy is the foremost of these. *Empathy* is the expression of caring and understanding of unresolved feelings. There are two main things that participants may have feelings about: the decision and the process of making the decision. Attending to these feelings can help repair any damage to group members' relationship to each other. This healing will help the group work together better when implementing the decision. It will also strengthen the long-term health of the group, building cohesion, cooperation, commitment and a more positive attitude.

While it is relatively simple in concept, empathy can be difficult to master. It is both a skill and an art. For empathy to be effective, it must be authentic. In other words, the person offering empathy must be willing to truly connect with the feelings they are empathizing with. You have to be comfortable and aware of your own feelings to be available for this type of connection. Having a good vocabulary for human needs is also helpful (see Figure 7.3, Universal Human Needs, in Chapter 7). Mastering empathy can be a lifelong project, but the power empathy has to improve relationships makes the effort to practice it very worthwhile. A more thorough understanding of empathy can be gleaned from Marshall Rosenberg's books on nonviolent communication.[1]

Group members can experience empathy in two ways. First, the facilitator may offer empathy to whomever needs it. This method does not require training the group in how to offer empathy to each other. Thus, it can be done quickly. It does require, however, that the facilitator possess strong empathy skills. The process can begin with the facilitator asking the

---

EMPATHY

Empathy is a very effective way of responding to another person's feelings.[2] Offering it to others helps them feel heard, understood, respected and cared for. It provides the message, "Your feelings make sense." When people hear this message, authentically delivered, a wonderful paradox occurs. Once feelings are genuinely understood, they often release or decrease in intensity. Meeting the need to be understood can be very satisfying and healing for both the giver and receiver of empathy.

To understand what empathy is, it helps to articulate what it is not. There are many possible reactions to the expression of feelings. Most are useful in some instances and problematic in other cases. Examples of responses that are not empathy are advice, reassurance, commiseration, blaming others, problem solving, contradicting, playing devil's advocate, distracting, theorizing, pitying, accommodating and recounting your own experiences. Empathy is also distinct from sympathy. Sympathy could be defined as "feeling sorry that someone else is feeling bad."

Empathy is "offering your understanding of another person's feelings." Expressions of empathy, therefore, start with the pronoun "you" not "I." Often people think they are being empathetic when they are really just trying to convince someone that they are being empathetic. "I really understand how you feel" is a statement about yourself. It is not empathy. Genuinely empathetic responses answer two key questions:

- How does this person feel?
- How does it make sense that they feel this way?

Consider, for instance, the challenge of responding to the following expression of feeling by a group member: "I'm just bummed because this plan won't even take effect until next summer." An example of empathy with this participant would be, "You feel disappointed about the group not

group, "Does anyone have any leftover feelings about the decision or the decision-making process?" As participants respond, the facilitator can attempt to empathize with each of them until some sense of satisfaction in being understood has been achieved.

Alternatively, the facilitator can assist group members to offer empathy to each other. Direct exchange of empathy between participants can generate a powerful healing of group relationships. More formal groups, however, may not be comfortable with the intensity of this process. Some may

---

choosing a solution that could be enacted more quickly. A fast response was a goal you had that did not get met." This statement describes both the feelings that were heard and an understanding of how those feelings make sense. Hearing this, the participant is likely to feel understood and cared about.

An example of a response that would not be empathy would be, "I know the solution we came up with might take longer, but I like to focus on how it may work better in the long run." This statement does not reflect the feeling heard and seems to be an indirect attempt to convince the participant to change their feelings. Hearing this, the participant is likely to feel a need to defend their disappointment.

In understanding why someone feels the way they do, it is useful to remember the important role human needs play in generating feelings. Emotions are primarily an indication of whether a person's needs are being met. When our needs are being met, we feel good. When our needs

are unmet, we feel a variety of negative feelings (such as frustration, anger, worry, fear, disappointment, sadness). The key, then, to understanding how a person feels is to identify the needs that underlie their emotions.

You can offer empathy by guessing about a person's feelings and the underlying needs that generate them. When guessing, it is important to respect that each person is the ultimate authority on her own feelings. If your guess is wrong, just stay open to any clarification you receive in response. Your guesses can use a simple template that clearly connects feelings with needs:

Are you feeling _____
because you sense a need for
_____ ?

Using this template in the above example might have produced the question, "Are you feeling disappointed because you sense a need for relief?"

eschew empathy as too touchy-feely. But when a group is willing and the facilitator sufficiently trained, sharing empathy can foster profound group bonding. Training in this type of facilitation, unfortunately, is beyond the scope of this book. It is best gained in an experiential training program, where facilitators-in-training can learn by watching, practicing and receiving direct feedback.

Ratify Acceptance of the Group Decision

After the group members have received empathy for any unresolved feelings, the group has the option of two more acts of closure. Not every group will appreciate the sense of closure these steps are designed to produce. Some participants may want to move on quickly once a decision has been made. People who are disappointed may not want to belabor the issue. A facilitator should therefore carefully assess whether the following two acts of closure are likely to improve group cohesion or annoy participants unnecessarily.

The first task is the ratification of the group decision. To accomplish this the facilitator addresses the group with some version of the following question:

> Does everyone accept that the group has made this decision
> in a fair process?

This question asks the participants to affirm that a legitimate process has taken place and that a decision resulting from it has been made. It should be very clear that this is not a second vote on the final proposal. That matter is already over.

- "So let me be really clear here. We are not voting again on the final proposal. That was already defeated. That's done. All I am asking now is if everyone accepts that the group has made this decision in a fair process. Does anyone object to the process we used?"

The purpose of this question is to help the group adjust to the finality of the decision. Those who opposed the final proposal may still object to the decision made (if it was passed). This question, however, asks them to agree that even though they opposed it, a legitimate decision was made. The empathy previously provided can help dissenters make this adjustment. It can soften any stubbornness or humiliation that may be a result of "losing." When asked to accept the result, these group members have a chance to drop their personal preference and acknowledge the will of the group as a whole.

The question does not need to be voted on. Asking people who oppose the decision to actively ratify it with a raised hand or voice vote may press the issue too much. It is usually enough to ask the question and pause to see if anyone raises an objection. If there are no objections, the facilitator moves on to the next step. And the group passes one more milestone in the decision-making process.

If someone does object, the facilitator must question the nature of the objection. Often, a participant may fail to understand the question. If that is not the problem, the facilitator should ask what about the process does the dissenter object to. Is there objection to the final decision rule? Is there objection to the facilitator's guidance? Is the dissenter simply needing to continue voicing opposition to the result, even though he understands that that is not the question? Regardless of the content of the objection, the facilitator can respond with empathy and ask the group (and the minutes) to note the point being made. Unless the group requires unanimity, the facilitator can then move on to the final act of closure.

Request Cooperation in Implementing the Decision

The final optional act of closure is a request for the group's cooperation as it implements whatever decision it has made. This request can be made by the facilitator, the person-in-charge or any motivated group member. The request asks everyone in the group to step up to the definition of egalitarian leadership offered in Chapter 3: thinking about the whole group. Regardless of whether a participant agrees with the decision the group has made, cooperation with its implementation is likely to be in the best interest of all. Undermining, sabotaging or passive-aggressively ignoring the decision are not tactics that promote healthy group functioning.

If someone remains opposed to a decision, they can represent their dissent honorably in two ongoing ways. First they can, over time, continue to educate group members about the reasons for their preference, in hopes of building support to reconsider the decision in the future. Second, if possible, they can propose that they not personally play a direct role in enacting the decision. The openness of this request allows the group to plan accordingly.

The final optional act of closure is a request for the group's cooperation as it implements whatever decision it has made.

The request for cooperation is not a demand that participants promise anything. It is made in order to help participants consciously choose how they will respond to the decision. This choice remains the prerogative of each participant. Making the request can motivate group members to choose to cooperate. But insisting on an answer can be counterproductive. Requiring a promise is often perceived as a coercive tactic. It can stir defiance. Usually it is better just to let the request be heard.

When resistance to the decision is high, a request for cooperation immediately after the decision may not be tactful. It may be best to give disappointed participants some time to adjust. Later, on an individual basis, a group leader can ask for cooperation if there is a need to do so.

Dealing with Unsatisfied Group Members

Sometimes a group member may continue to object to the decision or the decision-making process. This person may need some attention outside of the meeting to address their dissatisfaction. Otherwise she may not be cooperative with the implementation of the decision. The facilitator can handle the matter, or it can be delegated to an appropriate supervisor or fellow group member. The participant may need further help articulating her concerns. Or she may need more empathy. Sometimes disappointed participants need a way to recover a sense of feeling powerful. They may do this in their own way, or they may benefit from some personal attention.

A one-on-one conversation is often the best forum for dealing effectively with whatever the problem is. On occasion, a single group member may, with enough time, be able to identify a crucial aspect of the problem that the group has neglected. If so, this discovery may need to be brought back to the group. Alternatively, an individual may simply need sufficient attention before she is willing to re-engage a sense of cooperation. By supplying the needed attention to a group member outside of a meeting, the full group is spared a sometimes time-consuming process.

Occasionally, a group decision may cause a participant to question their willingness to continue in the group. This questioning might be resolved by addressing the feelings evoked in the decision-making process. Alternatively, the group's decision may become the catalyst for the participant to actually leave the group. Differences can be highlighted when decisions are made. And some group members may decide that they are no longer sufficiently in sync with the direction of the group. Changes such as this may not be due to any failure of the group or the individual leaving. They may just be a result of irreconcilable differences.

Concluding the Seven Steps

This final step of the CODM process concludes a substantial journey from topic suggestion to completed decision. The facilitator has guided the group through seven steps (or a shortcut version of CODM). The topic was framed carefully and then discussed openly. The stakeholders and all their concerns were identified to define the criteria for a satisfying solution. Root ideas were chosen, and the group collaboratively built proposal options on each one. Then, a direction was chosen, and the details of a final proposal were synthesized. Finally, the group reached a formal decision. This closure step also provided a way for the group to address any dissatisfaction remaining in any of the discussion participants. The process was participatory throughout, and it efficiently progressed toward the goal of generating as much agreement as possible. Congratulations! If you are here, you have performed a great service for your group.

Going For
Full Agreement
(Unanimity)

When a group can achieve unanimous agreement, the benefits are tremendous. The decision is likely to be well considered from multiple perspectives. The group is poised to cooperate well in implementation. And the atmosphere of the group is often buoyed by a sense of unity. So there is little question about the value of full agreement as a goal.

Some groups reach for this goal by using required unanimity as their final decision rule. Everyone must agree (or at least not block), or no proposal is approved. The Religious Society of Friends or Quaker faith is often cited as the modern origin of required unanimity. In the last 50 years, many organizations, including activist groups, collective businesses and intentional communities, have used it in a variety of settings. The cumulative experience of these groups has contributed to a greater understanding of how and when groups can achieve full agreement.

Unanimity and Consensus

As discussed in Chapter 1, requiring unanimity for decisions is commonly referred to as "consensus." To avoid confusion, however, the emerging discourse on the topic differentiates the decision rule (*unanimity*) from the decision-making process (*consensus*). A consensus process is a participatory discussion structure that attempts to generate as much agreement as possible. Virtually all groups that require unanimity use a consensus process. Groups that have other types of final decision rules, however, can also use a consensus process. They can thereby benefit from the increased levels of agreement a consensus process generates even if they don't require unanimity as the result.

Conditions That Favor Unanimity

The goals of requiring unanimity are only fully realized when a group is successful in reaching it. Thus, it is important to consider what conditions make full agreement more likely.[1] Here are some of the most important factors that improve the chances of successfully reaching unanimity:

- The smaller the group, the more easily full agreement can be reached.
- The more homogenous the group, the more easily full agreement can be reached.
- The group needs to have a clear common purpose.
- Participants must trust each other and value their relationships highly.
- Participants need to be trained to participate responsibly.
- Participants must put the best interest of the group before their own.
- Participants need to have enough time to spend in meetings.
- Skillful facilitation and agenda preparation are necessary.

These factors suggest that unanimity is most easily achieved in a small group of closely connected people who have similar values and share a common purpose for being in the group. Further, unanimity is more likely if these people have been trained in using a consensus process and all have the personal maturity to participate responsibly. They also will be more successful if they can devote sufficient time to meet and have a skillful facilitator.

Conversely, achieving unanimity is more challenging in groups that are larger, less intimate or more diverse. It is also more difficult when group members do not have the time, the training or the facilitation they need to succeed. It is particularly hard to reach unanimity when one or more participants have unresolved personal issues or high levels of mistrust or conflict. When any of these factors are present, even a very skillful facilitator cannot ensure that a consensus process will yield unanimous consent.

Process Tools to Reach Unanimity

There are several ways to structure a discussion to generate unanimity. Typically, they all involve a discussion period, which results in a proposal, and then a test for unanimity. If there is full agreement on the proposal, the process is complete. If not, dissenters are asked to speak their concerns so that the proposal can be modified or an alternative proposal can be developed. Each new version of a proposal is tested for unanimity until one succeeds. If no proposal achieves unanimous support, the issue is *put aside*, and the status quo remains in effect. The process typically follows this sequence:

1. Discuss any concerns.
2. Develop and clarify a proposal.
3. Test for level of agreement.
4. Repeat steps 1 to 3 as necessary (circle back).

These steps constitute the backbone of what is commonly called *consensus process*. Many adaptations of this basic outline have been formulated.[2] Some add steps or further clarify the basic steps. Some models require unanimity in step three for a proposal to pass. Others have a more flexible threshold of required agreement (unanimity minus one, unanimity minus two or a large supermajority are common). Understanding the distinction between the decision-making process and the final decision rule can help you identify how exisiting models actually vary.

Using CODM to Generate Full Agreement

Consensus-Oriented Decision-Making (CODM) is also built upon the consensus process outline. The word "oriented" is used to distinguish CODM from other consensus models. Though CODM shares the same basic values, there are two primary differences between CODM and other versions of consensus process. One is that CODM is considerably more detailed in its outline of how successful proposals can be collaboratively built. The other is that CODM is designed to be usable with any final decision rule. Unanimity is not integral to the process.

Nonetheless, CODM can be a very effective way to achieve unanimity whenever it is desired or required. Its detailed steps provide an efficient way to proceed whenever a proposal fails the test for unanimity. The facilitator can guide the group to circle back to an earlier step in order to recraft the final proposal. The objections raised by the participants opposed to the proposal determine which step to circle back to. There are several possible conditions:

- Is the objection centered on some detail of the proposal?
- If so, the group can circle back to Step 6 and reformulate the details of the final proposal until everyone agrees.

- Is the objection centered on a preference for a substantially different option?
- If so, the group can circle back to Step 5, choose a different option and then synthesize a new final proposal.

- Is the objection based on a preference for the status quo or existing policy?
- If so, the group can circle back to Step 4 and develop a proposal based on maintaining the status quo with whatever adaptations would improve it.

- Is the objection centered on a concern that has not been articulated?
- If so, the group can circle back to Step 3 and identify what concerns have been left out of the discussion.

- Is the objection centered on a concern that no existing options appear able to address?

- If so, the group can circle back to open discussion in order to generate new ideas about how to understand the problem and how to address it creatively.

- Is the objection based on whether the group is the appropriate body to be making a decision on this issue?
- If so, the group can circle back to Step 1 and clarify how the issue is framed and the goals for the group discussion.

The clarity of the CODM process can help increase a group's chances of successfully finding full agreement. A less-clear process can generate frustration within group members. Participants may become impatient when they do not understand how a discussion is structured or how further discussion will help them progress toward a decision. Even when a group needs to circle back, the clarity of the CODM steps can help a group continue with confidence and a sense of direction.

The clarity of the CODM process can help increase a group's chances of successfully finding full agreement.

Understanding the Meaning of Consent

It is also important to understand what it means to give consent. Considering the good of the whole group is strongly valued in consensus decision-making. Looking at the big picture and accepting responsibility for working with the group is encouraged. Group members may choose to use their vote to help the group come to a decision, rather than vote for their personal favorite option. Giving consent in this way indicates a willingness to accept the direction of the group over one's perceived self-interest.

Some facilitators promote this by suggesting a more relaxed standard of approval. In the discussion phase, each person is encouraged to voice their true feelings and preferences. But when it is time to vote, they are encouraged not to insist upon their personal favorite option. If everyone did this, unanimity might be very unlikely. Instead the participants are asked a version of, "Is this proposal something you can live with?" When participants vote to consent rather than voting their preference, proposals have a greater chance of passing. It can be unclear, however, what degree of support the passed proposal actually has.

CODM addresses this difficulty in the closure step. Two votes are held so that the vote to assess support for a proposal is separated from a vote to accept the group's decision. Participants can authentically vote their preference on the proposal, allowing an accurate measure of group support for the decision. Then, the facilitator can call for a vote to ratify acceptance of the group decision. At this point, even people who opposed the decision on the proposal can consent that the result is the will of the group.

Consensus Blocking

Most groups that require unanimity allow for the option of *consensus blocking*. Every group member retains the right to object to a proposal and single-handedly block a decision on it. The intention behind empowering each participant in this way is to ensure that the group cannot overlook the perspective of any member. Placing this power in each person's hands can help everyone participate with confidence that any fundamental concerns they have must be satisfied by any decision the group makes. This confidence can help free participants to address each other's concerns without fear that their own concerns will be sacrificed. No one has to worry about losing a vote because they were not politically savvy.

The power to block consensus, however, carries with it an important responsibility. If it is used inappropriately, consensus blocking can become a means for an individual to control a group. Therefore, groups that allow consensus blocking usually define guidelines for its use. Some of the common guidelines are:

- Limiting the option to block consensus to issues that are fundamental to the group's mission or potentially disastrous to the group.
- Providing an option for those who do not support a proposal to stand aside rather than block.
- Requiring two or more people to block for a proposal to be put aside.
- Require the blocking party to supply an alternative proposal or a process for generating one.

- Limiting each person's option to block consensus to a handful of times in one's life.

These guidelines are some of the options within the general ethics of consensus blocking. These ethics dictate that consensus blocking is to be used very sparingly. The good of the group should be the priority. Therefore, individuals should strive to cooperate with the general direction of a group. Both the group and those resistant to a proposal should try to deeply understand all perspectives in order to successfully formulate adaptations to a proposal. If someone's disagreement with a proposal is not based on a fundamental principle of the group, then they should consider *standing aside*. Their objection can be noted, without it blocking the decision. If a person does block a proposal, the ethics dictate that they should actively participate in formulating an alternative. Simply vetoing a decision is not considered a responsible use of consensus blocking.

Unfortunately, the ethics of consensus blocking can be difficult to clearly enforce. For instance, how does a group decide if an issue is "fundamental"? What would satisfy a blocking party's obligation to supply an alternative proposal? Who keeps track of how often a person blocks consensus? The facilitator can often resolve ambiguities by offering a clear description of the ethics of consensus blocking. Training the whole group in consensus process prior to a discussion can also head off problems. Sometimes, however, the appropriate use of consensus blocking remains controversial.

All decision rule options have their pros and cons; using a consensus-oriented process can mitigate these potential problems considerably.

Issues Arising from Consensus Blocking and Required Unanimity

All decision rule options have their pros and cons, as discussed in Chapter 3. Majority voting, for instance, can foster the formation of competitive factions and result in decisions that painfully ignore the concerns of a minority. Person-in-charge decision-making can foster very destructive power dynamics in a group. Using a consensus-oriented process can mitigate these potential problems considerably. But the potential for abuse of power exists in any group.

Experience has shown that requiring unanimity can also be problematic, particularly when full agreement is not achievable. Many groups have suffered through the agonizing fallout of failed attempts to require unanimity. The problems associated with this decision rule have even ended the existence of some groups. Since consensus decision-making has often been closely associated with the use of unanimity as a decision rule, an honest appraisal of potential drawbacks is important.

The analysis which follows is drawn from group experiences that I have personally witnessed. As a facilitator, I have helped many organizations reflect upon their group dynamics. Often, problems for which groups blamed themselves or group members have been successfully resolved simply by changing the requirement for unanimity to a decision rule that their group can more successfully attain.

If your group is deciding whether to use required unanimity, this account can help you make a more informed choice. If full agreement is not likely to be consistently attainable, these issues should be of concern. Following this analysis is a discussion of when required unanimity should be considered and how potential difficulties might be mitigated.

Ideological Issues

Ideological issues arise when the values that inspire the quest for unanimity are actually undermined by requiring it. Some of these values are described below. The discussion of each addresses some important paradoxes which anyone using the required unanimity decision rule should consider.

Widespread Agreement

Generating widespread agreement for any decision made is one important goal of requiring unanimity. Unfortunately, requiring unanimity does not ensure this. A decision not to make a change is a decision. In fact, when a group discusses a proposal and then puts it aside, it has decided to not implement it. Unless the choice to put it aside was unanimous, this decision is made without full agreement. When a popular proposal is blocked by a small minority of the group, the decision to put the issue aside actually enjoys very little agreement. In contrast, a majority vote decision is never made with less than 50% approval.

Requiring unanimity is usually intended to ensure *widespread agreement*. When unanimity is blocked by a small number of people, however, the group actually experiences *widespread disagreement* with the result. This widespread disagreement can have very toxic effects on the group dynamic going forward.

Equal Sharing of Power

Consensus blocking is often considered a way to equally share power in a group. Granting individuals an equal right to control the group's ability to make a decision, however, can be a very problematic way to provide equality. It necessitates that all group members have the ethics and maturity to use this power responsibly. This may not be a realistic expectation, particularly in groups with open membership. True equality may be better secured by a system that ensures that no group member ever has the power to individually control the group.

In practice, consensus blocking may offer a disproportionate amount of power to whomever supports the status quo. If just one or two people in a group object to a change for a fundamental reason, the preference of the rest can be blocked. In contrast, anyone who wants a change must convince the entire group to agree. This differential burden is contrary to the principle of equality.

Most groups that value consensus decision-making also value human diversity.

Authenticity

To reach unanimity, a group must value cooperation. But authenticity (honest communication) is usually an important value too. Requiring unanimity can potentially put these two values at odds. A group member may personally oppose a decision, but she may also want to cooperate with the group. At the end of a discussion, she may not feel free to vote her opposition because doing so would block the group. In order to cooperate, she must change her "No" vote to "Yes, I can live with it" or "I stand aside." In some cases, neither option feels authentic. Some people prefer to vote their true preference and accept the fact that their position may not win, rather than modify their vote to accommodate the group's goal to achieve unanimity.

The truth of existing disagreement is openly acknowledged in majority voting. In contrast, a requirement of unanimity sometimes suppresses the authentic acknowledgment of disagreement. Participants end up voting to cooperate rather than voting for their preferred proposal. Calling the result a unanimous decision can be a distortion, given the true degree of remaining disagreement.

Group Diversity

Most groups that value consensus decision-making also value human diversity. They recognize the contribution that the perspectives and talents of a wide variety of people can bring to a group. Many groups actively prioritize cultivating diversity in their group membership. It is important to look closely, therefore, at how requiring unanimity might actually discourage diversity.

A unanimous decision rule can result in a bias against welcoming group diversity. Groups that require unanimity may carefully screen new members. They understandably fear that open membership may make unanimity too hard to reach. As a group screens for similar values, however, it may also be reducing demographic diversity. The range of race, ethnicity, age, class, sexuality, psychological sophistication and other elements of diversity in the membership may decline.

Diverse group members may also feel less empowered to forward their own proposals in a group that requires unanimity. The chances of gaining universal support for a proposal that deviates significantly from the norm of the group culture may appear slim. People who differ broadly from the prevailing culture of the group are more likely to see proposals they initiate pass when the threshold necessary for approval is 51% rather than 100%.

The lower threshold supports a wider spectrum of approvable ideas. Thus, diverse group members may feel more empowered to influence a majority rule group than a group that requires unanimity.

Practical Issues

In addition to the ideological issues described above, some groups that require unanimity have experienced practical problems. It can take a group a long time to reach full agreement. Productive time spent in group discussion can improve group cohesion. But when discussion length becomes arduous, it can be counterproductive. Other issues arise when the group cannot make a decision or when widespread disagreement prevails because a popular proposal is blocked.

The group may not be able decide an issue that must be decided.
When the status quo is not an option, an issue cannot be put aside. Therefore, the group must make a decision. But if there is not unanimous consent, no decision can be made. The group is stuck. Group members in this situation may begin making decisions independently and cease functioning as a group.

The group may not be able to reach decisions on process issues.
When a group is conflicted about an issue, it may have to decide how to handle that issue (for instance: Should we keep discussing it? Should we vote? Should we send it to a committee? Is her block legitimate? Do we really need unanimity on this decision?). Unfortunately, the group may also be conflicted about the process question. When unanimity is required, but not available, the group may not be able to choose how to proceed.

The group may stagnate, unable to change and grow.
In a conflicted group, there may be little chance of passing new proposals or remaking outdated decisions. Thus, the status quo may remain in effect even if becomes less and less effective in meeting the needs of the group.

**The group may not be able to compete with other groups
that can make decisions quickly.**

Collective businesses that require unanimity may find themselves unable
to compete with rival businesses that can make decisions more efficiently.
Swift responses to shifts in market conditions may determine whether a
business succeeds or fails. The time necessary to generate unanimous consent for change may be a real disadvantage for a collective business.

The group's reputation in the community may suffer.

A slow decision-making process can be frustrating to members of the larger
community who do business with the group. Questions to the group can go
unanswered. The group can develop a reputation of being indecisive. Eventually the surrounding community members may avoid partnering with or
doing business with the group.

The group may lose talented members.

When people with high levels of personal effectiveness offer leadership,
they may expect an expedient time frame for decisions. Securing the unanimous support of the group, however, may require both personally ap-
pealing to members outside of meetings and then investing a lot of time
processing a decision in meetings. Many talented people prefer groups
where their contributions are more easily approved and they can get right
to work.

The group may try to evict a member.

Some group members may try to expel participants who tend to block or
slow the group down. Usually this effort begins indirectly. On the surface,
the group may act like everyone cares about each other. Meanwhile, underneath the surface, people are desperately hoping certain group members
will leave. There may be strategies designed to get a group member to resign
voluntarily. Or, a direct effort to scapegoat and expel a group member may
surface.

Discussions may die before they begin.

Sometimes groups that require unanimity will claim that consensus blocking is rarely a factor because it is almost never practiced. Unfortunately, a closer look may tell a different story. When everyone knows that someone in the group is strongly opposed to an idea, the topic will often not come up for discussion. Why spend hours discussing something you know is never going to gain unanimous agreement? People faced with this choice may prefer to avoid the acute disappointment that carrying a doomed proposal to a vote would bring.

Agonizing discussions may be repeated in subsequent meetings.

When a popular proposal has been defeated by a small minority of the group, the proposal's proponents may want to try again. This can result in the repetition of an agonizing and unsuccessful discussion. Some groups prevent this by determining a minimum time interval before a topic can be revisited (i.e., six months, one year, three years). In the meantime, however, the group may experience high levels of disagreement with existing policy.

Participants who can endure conflict for longer may prevail.

Unfortunately, decision-making sometimes is affected by the group's frustration with the length of a discussion. Thus, those participants who can endure conflict for longer have a greater chance of winning concessions from those who tire quickly. When groups are split, it is sometimes this factor, rather than deeper understanding and collaboration, that determines the resulting decision. More obstinate participants may more frequently get their way.

Founders may wield greater power than newcomers.

The status quo is highly protected by a unanimous decision rule. Thus, the decisions made by the group's founders can be very difficult to change. Newcomers may feel unable to make the group their own. Groups sometimes find that new people join, stay for a short period and then leave when they realize how little influence they can have on the group.

Attention seekers may dominate the focus of the group.

Some people enjoy the attention of a group. They may find that raising objections to a proposal is an easy way to become the focus of group attention. Everyone needs them to agree. Therefore, their vote may be courted with both attention and other forms of appeasement. Meanwhile, the efficiency of the group process can suffer.

Mavericks may defy the group.

Those who don't want to get stuck in a long group process may adopt a maverick style. They pursue independent initiatives without approval from the main group. Tension between mavericks and group leaders is common, but mavericks can usually tolerate unresolved conflict. Mavericks may draw moral authority to ignore the group process from a belief that the power dynamics behind the consensus blocking process are unjust.

Special committees may take over decision-making.

Some groups have responded to long, arduous unanimity seeking discussions by establishing a steering committee (or leadership council) charged with making decisions on behalf of the group. This two-tiered approach may effectively improve decision-making efficiency. Using a two-tiered system, however, reduces the broader participation of group members in decision-making. And some members may feel disenfranchised. While two-tiered systems can work well, groups should consider whether a one-tiered system that did not require unanimity might also improve efficiency without reducing the participation of the full group.

Groups that use required unanimity should be aware of these potential ideological and practical issues. When unanimity is achievable, they are not likely to manifest. The potential for dysfunction increases, however, when decisions are blocked by small minorities or the decision-making process

Requiring a consensus process, rather than requiring unanimity, can offer a group substantial protection.

is protracted. The very values behind a group's choice to require unanimity are sometimes undermined when an attempt at unanimity fails. Practical problems also have the potential to outweigh benefits. Thus, any group considering required unanimity for ideological reasons should carefully consider the issues described above. And any group experiencing problems should consider whether a change in their decision rule might improve the situation.

As an alternative to requiring unanimity as a decision rule, a group can require the use of a consensus process. The bylaws or operating agreements can specify that the group utilize a consensus decision-making process for all major decisions. Requiring the use of a consensus process (without requiring unanimity) can offer a group substantial protection from the dangers of majority vote or person-in-charge decision rules. And it can do this without risking the problems associated with consensus blocking.

When Should a Group Require Unanimity?

Even though there are potential problems associated with it, required unanimity is sometimes the best choice for a decision rule. It can supply vital motivation for participants to try hard to reach full agreement and to consistently use a consensus process. It can also offer an important message to all participants that their perspective will not be overlooked by the group. These can be valuable contributions to an atmosphere of collaboration and strong group cohesion.

Two questions are important for any group considering required unanimity. First, "Is full agreement attainable in your group without sacrificing other important values?" In other words, can your group succeed in finding full agreement without experiencing the difficulties outlined above? If so, your group may be able to successfully use required unanimity and thereby boost your group's sense of unity.

Secondly, some groups may need to ask, "Is required unanimity the only real option?" Unanimity is sometimes the only way to secure a group's survival or the success of its mission. For example, vital participants may not enter a discussion, or essential members will not join a group, without an agreement to require unanimity. Some of the factors that necessitate requiring unanimity are listed below:

- Essential members will not participate without an agreement to require unanimity.
- Requiring unanimity provides an essential sense of group cohesion.
- The stakes of a decision are so high that unanimity is essential.
- Successful implementation of a decision requires complete, unanimous support.
- The group cannot agree to any other decision rule.

Common Usages

There are numerous illustrative examples of groups that successfully require unanimity. As noted in Chapter 3, the permanent members of the United Nations Security Council all have consensus blocking power. The necessity of the participation of all parties, the high stakes of their decisions and the need for full cooperation in implementing their decisions all make required unanimity an appropriate decision rule for this group.

Trial juries also often operate under required unanimity. The combination of careful jury selection and a small number of participants makes unanimity usually achievable. The high stakes of administering true justice make unanimous decisions useful. Unanimity provides a greater sense of resolution and increases public confidence in the resulting verdicts. Additionally, the availability of a retrial (expensive though it may be) provides a fallback option when unanimity cannot be reached.

Other common usages of required unanimity are in intentional communities, collective businesses and nonprofit groups. When these groups are small enough, have well-aligned values and are committed to the time and training required to responsibly operate within the ethics of consensus blocking, they may find that requiring unanimity works well for them. The attention they pay to building close and cooperative relationships with each other usually provides the basis for this success. The requirement of unanimity provides an ongoing reminder to maintain the group relationships well enough for unanimity to be achievable on a consistent basis.

The highest levels of agreement are reached when a participatory process is used in combination with a decision rule that allows a group to make a decision with whatever level of agreement it has been able to attain.

Judicious Use of Required Unanimity

Sometimes groups designate different decision rules for different types of decisions. Simple majority, for instance, may be the decision rule for routine decisions, while unanimity may be required for more fundamental decisions. This distinction can help a group operate efficiently on a daily basis while protecting a sense of unity regarding its primary mission. Requiring unanimity offers strong protection for the status quo. Thus, it is a useful way to solidify decisions that spring from the core values of the group's founders. While there may be a drawback in the lack of flexibility this allows for new members to shape the group, it may offer a desirable sense of security to the group's founders. It is important, whenever a group has different decision rule options, that the criteria determining which option should apply is clearly understood.

Establishing a Fallback Decision Rule

When a group does require unanimity, it should consider the option of a fallback decision rule. A fallback option can address many issues sometimes associated with requiring unanimity. It provides a means for a group to make decisions whenever it needs to, even if it cannot reach full agreement. Common fallback options include supermajority votes, majority votes or delegating decisions to a committee.

With a fallback option, a group can benefit from the motivation provided by the primary decision rule (required unanimity). A consensus process can be employed to reach as much agreement as possible. If full agreement is not reached in a reasonable time frame, however, the group can fall back to its secondary decision rule and complete the decision-making process.

For some people, this combination offers a good marriage of ideology and practicality. The group can be officially aligned with the goals of a consensus process, but can still make decisions when it cannot reach unanimity. For others, the notion of a fallback rule is doublespeak. They point out that whatever rule a group ultimately falls back on is its "true" decision rule. To avoid this paradox, some groups choose to require the use of a consensus process with a supermajority decision rule. This can avoid the confusion sometimes created by requiring unanimity, but also having a fall-back decision rule.

Summary

This discussion has attempted to shed light on the pros and cons of requiring unanimity. Under the right conditions, requiring unanimity can work well and provide a group with a strong motivation to seek full agreement. On the other hand, many groups using this decision rule have suffered problems from not being able to make decisions when they needed to or suffered from widespread disagreement caused by a blocked decision. This is a sad result for a group whose goal is actually the opposite, making decisions with maximum agreement.

Whether or not your group chooses to require unanimity, a consensus decision-making process can help you find as much agreement as you can. If your group requires unanimity, it can use a consensus process to try to get there. Another option is for your group to require the use of a consensus process (rather than require unanimity as a decision rule). No rule or process, however, can ensure that all people will agree. The highest levels of agreement are reached when a participatory process is used in combination with a decision rule that allows a group to make a decision with whatever level of agreement it has been able to attain.

Resources for Facilitators

Facilitating groups can be incredibly rewarding. When you are successful, your efforts can be a great help to the group members you meet with. You help decisions get made. But you also help relationships deepen. You help creativity emerge. And you help participants in conflict find resolution and peace. As the group's work impacts the world around it, your contribution radiates outward.

Such important work can be challenging. There are many facets to facilitating groups. The varying demands of the role require that facilitators keep learning more about groups and about themselves. Experience is a valuable teacher. But learning from others is important as well. Here are some resources available for your continued education.

Author Websites

The following websites, maintained by the author, host a regularly updated list of resources valuable for continuing education in consensus decision making and group facilitation.

A Virtual Learning Center for People Interested in Making Decisions by Consensus: ConsensusDecisionmaking.org

This public service website hosts articles and videos from many different authors about consensus decision-making. The site is dedicated to fostering ongoing discussion about what consensus is and how it works. Various models and approaches are included. The site also features a directory of facilitators and trainers who use consensus. Trainings and workshops throughout the world are listed on the events page. Organizations that use consensus decision-making are also indexed on the site. Contributions to the site are welcome.

Hiring a CODM Facilitator: GroupFacilitation.net

This website describes my services as a professional facilitator and trainer. If you want to hire an outside facilitator, this site may help you see if I might be able to help. Additional articles on the CODM process are also available on this site.

Appendix: CODM Crib Sheet

Step 1: Framing the Topic

1. Collect agenda items.
2. Clarify the essence, goals and appropriate process for each issue.
3. Interview a sample of group members.
4. Identify and delegate useful pre-meeting research.
5. Introduce the discussion.

Step 2: Open Discussion

1. Inspire an open-minded, creative discussion.
2. Provide guidelines and structure for the discussion.
3. Manage the discussion.
4. Support full and varied participation.
5. Record the ideas generated on an Ideas Chart.

Step 3: Identifying Underlying Concerns

1. Ask the group to identify all the stakeholders affected by the issue.
2. List all underlying concerns of each stakeholder on an Underlying Concerns Chart.
3. Gather all the identified concerns to form the basis for collaborative proposal development.

Step 4: Collaborative Proposal Development

1. Describe the collaborative process of taking turns to build multiple proposals.
2. Help the group select root ideas on which to develop proposals.
3. Use a Proposal Development Chart to help the group develop each option to its full potential.

Step 5: Choosing a Direction

1. Check for readiness to choose a direction.
2. Analyze the proposal options.
3. Use preference gradient voting to choose which option to develop further.

Step 6: Synthesizing a Final Proposal

1. Review any unsatisfied concerns.
2. Identify details that might improve the proposal.
3. Select which details to include in the proposal.
4. Compose final wording for the proposal and a process for deciding any unresolved details.

Step 7: Closure

1. Apply the group's final decision rule.
2. Optional: Provide empathy for any unsatisfied participants.
3. Optional: Ratify acceptance of the group decision.
4. Optional: Request cooperation in implementing the decision.

Notes

Introduction

1. To protect the confidentiality of actual groups, the details of these examples have been changed. The resulting vignettes are not intended to be representative of any existing organization.

Chapter 1

1. This chart is adapted from a similar one in Sam Kaner et al.'s *Facilitator's Guide to Participatory Decision-Making* (Jossey-Bass, 2007).

Chapter 2

1. This discussion of facilitative leadership is built upon the work of Roger Schwarz in his book, *The Skilled Facilitator* (Jossey-Bass, 2002).

Chapter 3

1. This outline of decision rules options is built upon the discussion in Sam Kaner et al.'s *Facilitator's Guide to Participatory Decision-Making* (Jossey-Bass, 2007).

Chapter 6

1. See the Institute of Cultural Affairs in the U.S.A. website: ica-usa.org.
2. R. Brian Stanfield, ed. *The Art of Focused Conversation: 100 Ways to Access Group Wisdom in the Workplace*. New Society, 2000.
3. See the Center for Nonviolent Communication website: cnvc.org.
4. See Dynamic Facilitation Associates website: tobe.net.
5. See Open Space World website: openspaceworld.org.

Chapter 7

1. See Open Space World website: openspaceworld.org.
2. This discussion of positions vs. underlying concerns is built upon the work of Roger Fisher and William L. Ury in their book, *Getting to Yes: Negotiating Agreement Without Giving In* (Penguin, 1991).

3. This discussion of human needs is drawn from the work of Marshall Rosenberg in the book, *Non-Violent Communication: A Language of Life* (Puddledancer Press, 2003).

Chapter 9

1. Sam Kaner et al. originally describe a similar voting process, "gradients of agreement" in *Facilitator's Guide to Participatory Decision-Making* (Jossey-Bass, 2007).

Chapter 11

1. See resource list for details.
2. This discussion of empathy is built upon the work of Marshall Rosenberg in the book, *Non-Violent Communication: A Language of Life* (Puddledancer Press, 2003).

Chapter 12

1. Diana Leafe Christian offers a useful discussion of the factors affecting a group's likelihood of success in reaching full consent in her book, *Creating a Life Together* (New Society Publishers, 2003).
2. One popular version of a basic consensus process model is outlined in the book by CT Lawrence Butler and Amy Rothstein, *On Conflict and Consensus* (Food Not Bombs Publishing, 2006).

Index

A

active listening. *See* reflective listening.
advocate system, 101
agenda items, 53–58
authenticity, 147–148
authority figures, 25. *See also* executive committee; person-in-charge.

B

brainstorming, 70
breakout groups, 75–76

C

card storming, 79, 72
charting, 82–83, 87, 94, 102–106, 116–117
clarification, of issue, 55–58
closure, 45, 129–137
collaboration, 5, 7, 14, 20, 42–43, 52, 97–106
committees, 2, 9, 33, 45–48, 87, 126–127, 152. *See also by name.*
communication, 3–4, 28, 54, 55, 57, 67, 75. *See also* authenticity; reflective listening.
concerns
    underlying, 85–95
    unsatisfied, 122–123
conflict, 4, 14, 26, 58, 60, 63, 66, 130, 149, 151, 152
consensus, and unanimity, 2–3, 139–140, 152
consensus blocking, 144–145
consensus process, 141
consent, 143–144
content, vs. process, 17
critical analysis, 70, 109–112
criticism, reframing, 71

163

About the Author

Amy Cooper

Tim Hartnett is a professional group facilitator, mediator and family therapist in Santa Cruz, CA. He earned a PhD in psychology, researching methods for facilitating high-conflict families in divorce. Tim then taught group process on the faculty of John F. Kennedy University. He brings his training in conflict resolution and nonviolent communication to enhance the practice of group facilitation in a variety of settings. He is a member of the International Association of Facilitators and the National Coalition for Dialogue & Deliberation. Tim's work has been motivated by a lifelong interest in cooperative groups and consensus decision-making. Tim's practice, Consensus Facilitation, can be accessed through his website: GroupFacilitation.net.

If you have enjoyed *Consensus-Oriented Decision-Making*,
you might also enjoy other

BOOKS TO BUILD A NEW SOCIETY

Our books provide positive solutions for people who want to
make a difference. We specialize in:

**Sustainable Living • Green Building • Peak Oil
Renewable Energy • Environment & Economy
Natural Building & Appropriate Technology
Progressive Leadership • Resistance and Community
Educational & Parenting Resources**

New Society Publishers

ENVIRONMENTAL BENEFITS STATEMENT

New Society Publishers has chosen to produce this book on recycled paper made with
100% post consumer waste, processed chlorine free, and old growth free.

For every 5,000 books printed, New Society saves the following resources: [1]

24	Trees
2,141	Pounds of Solid Waste
2,356	Gallons of Water
3,073	Kilowatt Hours of Electricity
3,893	Pounds of Greenhouse Gases
17	Pounds of HAPs, VOCs, and AOX Combined
6	Cubic Yards of Landfill Space

[1]Environmental benefits are calculated based on research done by the Environmental Defense Fund and
other members of the Paper Task Force who study the environmental impacts of the paper industry.

For a full list of NSP's titles, please call 1-800-567-6772 *or check out our website* at:

www.newsociety.com

NEW SOCIETY PUBLISHERS